R.F.K. '68

R.F.K. '68

THE SOUNDS OF TIME

LEON WOLF FAINSTADT

RFK'68
THE SOUNDS OF TIME

iUniverse books may be ordered through booksellers or by contacting:

iUniverse
1663 Liberty Drive
Bloomington, IN 47403
www.iuniverse.com
1-800-Authors (1-800-288-4677)

Because of the dynamic nature of the Internet, any web addresses or links contained in this book may have changed since publication and may no longer be valid. The views expressed in this work are solely those of the author and do not necessarily reflect the views of the publisher, and the publisher hereby disclaims any responsibility for them.

Any people depicted in stock imagery provided by Thinkstock are models, and such images are being used for illustrative purposes only. Certain stock imagery © Thinkstock.

ISBN: 978-1-4917-4571-7 (sc)
ISBN: 978-1-4917-4572-4 (e)

Printed in the United States of America.

iUniverse rev. date: 10/29/2014

TO _____

_____

LEON WOLF FAINSTADT

"THE SOUNDS OF TIME"

OUR GROUP ON STAGE AT THE EMBASSY BALLROOM THE LOS
ANGELES TIMES JUNE 5, 1968 COVER LEON IS NEXT TO THE ABC
CAMERA, KRIS DESATEL THEN JIM WOLK ON GUITAR.

FIVE MINUTES PRIOR TO SENATOR KENNEDY'S VICTORY SPEECH

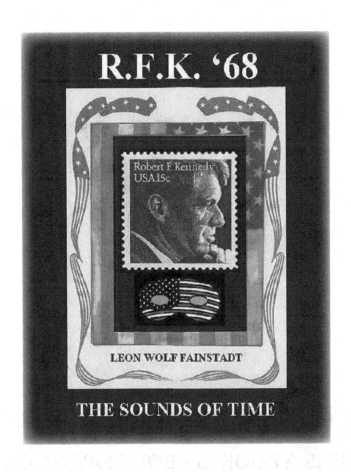

R.F.K.'68/THE SOUNDS OF TIME

THE ADVANCE SINGING GROUP FOR SOUTHERN CALIFORNIA IN THE RACE FOR THE PRESIDENCY OF 1968

AUTHOR: LEON WOLF FAINSTADT

BORN ON JUNE 5, 1945 IN A SLAVE LABOR CAMP IN SIBERIA.

THIS BOOK IS ABOUT A CAMPAIGN AND

<u>MY ATTEMPT TO SAVE THE LIFE OF SEN. ROBERT F. KENNEDY</u>

THIS BOOK IS 46 YEARS IN THEMAKING.

"SWANSTARZ" (BOBBY WOULD HAVE LIKED THIS BOOK)

SWANSTARZ IS A BOOK IS ABOUT SAVING OUR PLANET

ONE BIG RIPPLE OF HOPE.

R.F.K. '68

R.F.K.'68

INSIDE THE LAST CAMPAIGN

OF SENATOR ROBERT F. KENNEDY

AT THE AMBASSADOR HOTEL

AS TOLD BY THE AUTHOR

LEON WOLF

FAINSTADT

Germany-1947

Mendel/Leon Fajnstadt

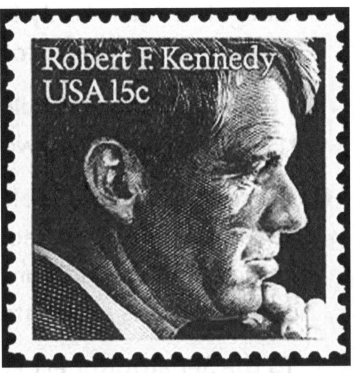

Robert F. Kennedy
USA 15c

TWO COURAGEOUS MEN IN MY LIFE

MY FATHER, MENDEL, AND BOBBY KENNEDY

FOR

Janet, my wife, and Rachele, my daughter

who begged me to write this Book.

They heard the story a hundred times.

To my parents who endured the Nazi onslaught in Poland only to be put in a Soviet Gulag for six years from 1939 to 1945.

For the Six Million and Millions of others who perished in World War Two. SHALOM / PEACE

Dr. Jayson I. Sher who took photographs after the assassination and kept them in a sealed container, unopened, for 46 years. Many of his photographs are contained in this book.

To the Senator Robert F. Kennedy family who continue creating value for America and the world. Especially to Mrs. Ethel Kennedy and Jerry Bruno who picked my group, "The Sounds of Time", to be the advance singing group for The Southern California's RFK Presidential Campaign.

To Caroline Kennedy and her father President John F. Kennedy, who I met in Santa Monica. I met him two months before the Cuban Missile Criisis in August 19, 1962 when I was 17 years old.

To the hundreds of millions of people that President John F. Kennedy and Senator Robert F. Kennedy saved by preventing a nuclear war with the Soviet Union. To the extended families who owe their lives to the courageous actions of both J.F.K. and R.F.K. two amazing human beings.

To Vasily Arkhipov, of the Soviet Union, who did not fire his nuclear missiles as his submarine came under attack by American warships. His courage, along with the Kennedy's, John and Robert, prevented a catastrophic nuclear war in 1962. See the <u>Movie 13 Days</u> and you will understand how close we came to living back in the stone age.

Pray we may see human beings of this caliber again.

©

THE AMERICAN FLAG MASK WAS FIRST DESIGNED IN 1990
BY THE FREEDOM TRAIL CORP. I CREATED IT IN SUPPORT
OF AMERICAN EDUCATION. CREATED AS A LOGO WHICH
WAS EASILY IDENTIFIABLE AND USED BY "CHAMPIONS" OF
ALL CHILDREN IN AMERICA. TWO CHAMPIONS, MALE AND
FEMALE, WEAR THE MASK TO CREATE HEROIC FIGURES.

IN KEEPING WITH CREATING "RIPPLES OF HOPE" IT IS MY
BELIEF THAT ONLY THROUGH EDUCATION CAN THERE
BE A LEVEL PLAYING FIELD FOR ALL AMERICANS.

CURRENTLY THERE ARE PROBLEMS ACROSS AMERICA
IN WHICH CHILDREN AND ADULTS SUFFER. FINANCIAL
DISPARITIES. THE ENVIRONMENT SUFFERS FROM THE
INDIFFERENCE OF CAPTAINS OF INDUSTRY WHO DESTROY
MOUNTAINS AND RIVERS WITH ABANDON FOR MONEY.

FROM THAT SAD DAY IN 1968 TO THE PRESENT I HAVE
PRAYED FOR GUIDANCE ON HOW TO CREATE VALUE WITH
MY LIFE. ALL EFFORTS MOVE TOWARDS CREATING RIPPLES
OF HOPE. ROBERT F. KENNEDY IS MY CHAMPION.

SAVING OUR PLANET FROM THE HORRIBLE DESTRUCTION
OF A NUCLEAR WAR SHOULD BE THE DECISIVE FACTOR.
YOU'RE HERE BECAUSE THEY WERE HERE.

PLEASE LEARN ABOUT HAYM SALOMON

HE SAVED GEORGE WASHINGTON'S ARMY AND SUPPLIED MONEY TO THE REVOLUTION WHENEVER IT WAS NEEDED.

HE WAS COURAGEOUS, GENEROUS, AND JEWISH.

PRESIDENT WASHINGTON NEVER FORGOT HIM.

George Washington gave a speech where he stated

The Jewish people would always be welcome in America.

I believe the generosity of Haym Salomon had a lot to do with that.

The Kennedy's saved us. All of us.

Who will save us next time.

Something tells me it will be WOMEN.

Our planet is functioning at 50%. Can you imagine 100%

JUNE 4, 1968

FOR WHOM HE SAVED THE UNION
THE MEMORY OF ABRAHAM LINCOLN
IS ENSHRINED FOREVER

I SPOKE WITH JACK SMITH A COLUMNIST FOR THE L.A. TIMES ON JUNE 4, 1968. ONE DAY BEFORE THE PRIMARY

"HE REMINDS ME OF ABRAHAM LINCOLN"

AUTHOR'S STATEMENT

I was named after my grandfather – LION WOLF IN A GOOD CITY. I am an abstract artist and this is my second book. I write like an artist. Just like a painting you can open to any page and be at the beginning. My intention is to paint a picture of what I experienced as a young man working for a dear human being named Robert Frances Kennedy. I met President John F. Kennedy when I was 17 at the beach in Santa Monica, two months before the Cuban Missile Crisis. The Kennedy's saved us. They saved you and all of the world. This is a series of snap shots. Please say a prayer for the Kennedy brothers. I love sharing my experiences and they are numerous. Unbelievable at times. Read on.

BORN IN SIBERIA IN A SLAVE LABOR CAMP

Imagine being born in a slave labor camp, in Siberia, where the weather is -50 degrees and where only a "one-legged chicken" keeps you alive. Yes that chicken layed an egg each day and that was my salvation. My mother was astonished that the chicken kept laying an egg on schedule each day.

Upon escaping from Siberia, in a hay covered wagon, we found a convoy of American Soldiers who gave us a ride through Europe. I still remember the sadness in the eyes of those soldiers who sat across from me.

We settled in Paris, France near the Bastille. Life was not easy but it was life. My father began falling. He fell in the apartment and then fell in the street unconscious. He was seen by a doctor who discovered he had a brain tumor. He needed an brain operation. My mother was more than distraught.She was very angry and did not hide her disappointment. He died at the young age of 39.

In France it rains a lot and when the thunder and lightning began Rose would abandon my brother Jack and I, at the dinner table, and run into a closet to hide. My mother, Rose, was reliving the bombing she experienced on September 1, 1939 when the Nazi's attacked Poland. Her parents were dead, and now, she was losing a husband. Mendel did not survive the operation but he was fearless and taught me about courage before he died in 1950. He is buried in Banolet, France. I prayed at his burial site when I was 39 which was the same age as when he died. It was mystic. Friends from his hometown paid for the burial. Finding his grave on a Sunday in France was miraculous.

We left Bremerhaven, Germany on the USS General Blatchford. On that voyage I danced on table tops for eggs. There was that egg again. People gave us their eggs. My good friend Elliot Gilbert and I came on that ship together along with Elliot's mother, father, and brother Jack. We landed at Ellis Island on Thanksgiving Week. We thought all Americans ate like this all the time.

I have tried to live my life with courage and sensitivity. I have had people point guns, shotguns, rifles at me, knives pointed at me and never felt fear. I have lived without fear as my father taught me. He was the angel watching over me. My father has always been my "spirit guide" and my protector. You have no idea how many impossible situations I have encountered and come out protected. Getting hit by a tow truck was one such experience. I was in a car.

The book I wrote is about my experience working in the Presidential Campaign of Senator Robert F. Kennedy. I pray for him every day. When I drive by the former site of the Ambassador Hotel I pray for him. I had visited the Ambassador, when it stood, at least 30 times. I walked the halls, the pantry, the kitchen, I closed the doors, of the Colonial room, and prayed for him and asked him for guidance on how to live my life. I have never stopped asking for guidance. Last week I had three nights of dreams in a row where I was having a conversation with him. I told him what I was doing and it was truly amazing.

Some of the experience I shared with you will be very difficult to understand for many readers. Try harder. We are all miracles. Whenever someone has a problem or difficulty I always say: Go feed the world. Make a person. Try to make just one person! There is not enough money in the entire world for that to happen. So we must treat each other as miracles. You are a miracle.

Once a young man, in San Francisco, pointed a gun at me. I did not even know him so I asked him what he was doing. He just stood there with that gun pointed at my head. I finally asked him to either shoot or put the gun away and that I was not afraid of him. He put it away and I took him out to breakfast with his girlfriend. I told him at breakfast that he needed professional help and made him promise to see a doctor. He promised and they left.

In junior high school in East Los Angeles, where I grew up, a kid came up to me in the hallway and pointed a knife at my neck. He asked for a dime. I looked at him and told him I would give him a quarter if he promised not to do this again and he promised. It was that kind of rough neighborhood then in 1957.

I went on to bigger experiences. I wanted to create value especially after Sen. Robert F. Kennedy was assassinated on June 5th my birthday. Since June 5, 1968 I have challenged myself to become a better person. There is still time for that.

I am currently working on "SWANSTARZ" which is currently in book form and the goal is for a major film on the environment. We must save planet earth. It might be easier than we think. We are all in this together. Some need coaxing.

SWANSTARZ.COM

A CHILDRENS BOOK FOR ADULTS

TO SAVE THE ENVIRONMENT AND OUR PLANET

The idea for the book and film project came out of an abstract painting. It was a gift for me to work with. It is about Swans and Heroic characters from the Milky Way who come to earth to protect our children and the future of mankind.

You see not protecting our environment is like exploding 50 nuclear weapons. The explosions are over time but the result is the same.

In this book/film Swanstarz is a brother/sister group who have extraordinary powers. They fight evil without violence. That is worth saying again: Listen: THEY FIGHT EVIL WITHOUT VIOLENCE!

Think on that. How is that possible? The champions from the Milky Way can change into Swans. So they are both beautiful and powerful.

Bobby would have loved that.

<u>FOREWORD</u>

The style of this book was created as if I were doing an abstract painting. In this style one can open to any part of the book and be at the beginning. When one is looking at a Jackson Pollack there is no starting point for the viewer. You just start looking.

Senator Robert F. Kennedy was an amazing human being with a beautiful family and a great wife. He said when questioned why he was running he said it was not for the money. He had enough from his family to live a quiet comfortable life. He challenged himself throughout his life.

I was fortunate to have met President Kennedy in 1962 on August 19th. He was all smiles as the crowd around him went wild. In 1968 I connected to Sen. Robert F. Kennedy at the Los Angeles Sports Arena. The SRO event was filled with 15,000 Kennedy fans. I found a way to make a connection by standing still and allowing him to see me standing 10 yards from the stage. I held up a peace sign and he returned the jesture and smiled.

My uncle and future father were constantly marching for something in Poland. They were very political. One day my uncle went out and never came back. His name was Moses. My mother warned me to stay away from politics but I just enjoyed campaigning. I walked for miles and rang door bells. Gave out pamphlets for Ed Roybal and campaigned for Governor Brown. I loved it.

Working on the Kennedy campaign was the highest and one of the lowest moments in my life. I must have told my story about THE SOUNDS OF TIME at least hundreds of times.

I HAVE HAD MIRACULOUS EXPERIENCES THAT I FELT EVERYONE HAD. KNOWING SOMEONE BY JUST LOOKING AT A PHOTOGRAPH HAPPENED MANY TIMES IN MY LIFE. EVEN KNOWING THE NAMES OF PEOPLE I HAD NEVER MET OCCURRED MANY TIMES.

I AM TELLING YOU THIS AT THE OUTSET SINCE YOU WILL COME ACROSS THE STORY OF LOOKING AT A YOUNG MAN IN A PHOTO, THAT I HAD

NEVER SEEN OR HEARD OF BEFORE AND STATING THE THIS MAN WOULD
BECOME PRESIDENT. HOW DOES THAT WORK?

STARING DOWN PEOPLE WHO HAD KNIVES, HANDGUNS, PISTOLS, AND
NEVER ONCE FEELING AFRAID. DON'T ASK ME HOW THIS WORKS. IT WAS
JUST PART OF MY D.N.A. THIS IS THE TRUTH. TALKING PEOPLE DOWN
FROM THEIR RAGES.

After working for Senator Robert Kennedy I took on large projects and
challenged myself. One such project was to keep New York City from
going bankrupt. Billboards went up in New York and Los Angeles and
letters went to President Ford to change his mind about letting the city go
bankrupt. This was my Kennedy moment.

That year I went to Las Vegas to meet with Frank Sinatra at Caesars
Palace. I had a letter of introduction form his friend and had a packet of
information regarding the effort to save N.Y. His secretary would not even
take it. I had just enough money to fly to Vegas, give him the package, and
return to Los Angeles. Since the secretary would not take it I SLEPT ON
THE DESERT ON A PIECE OF CARDBOARD until the next day. Frozen stiff.

The next day, through his friend, I found out where he was eating after
his show. In a foolish act of bravado I challenged his friend Jilly Rizzo so I
could get the package of information to him. Because things were getting
loud Mr. Sinatra looked over and told Jilly to let me come over to him. He
loved it. He invited me to his show, front center, and before he started
his performance asked me to stand up and then he said: LADIES AND
GENTLEMEN MEET LEON FAINSTADT. HE IS GOING TO SAVE NEW YORK.
The applause was amazing. He just smiled and held up a poster we had
created. I spent the next two nights at the show. Persistence paid off. New
York was eventually saved from bankruptcy. THAT WAS BOBBY KENNEDY.

Every day since June 5, 1968 I have tried to live my life to create value.
Visited the White House, the Dept. of Education, Sen. Rockefeller's office.
By the way when we came to America one of our dear cousins told my
mother to ask Rockefeller for help since she was not about to.

Our singing group, THE SOUNDS OF TIME, performed for tens of thousands of people as we criss-crossed Los Angeles and Orange County.

As I was getting close to finishing this book I had a series of dreams in which I had conversations with Senator Kennedy. He looked great and it felt like 1968 and there was a lot of energy in those dreams.

I have had those kind of dreams with my grandparents who died before I was born and were buried along the train tracks, in a forest, in Siberia. My mother cried when she heard one of those dreams and she was crying because I described what they were wearing when they died and the fact that my grandmother was incapable of speaking. My mother had been too embarrassed to discuss this part of her life. She was happy for me.

Bobby Kennedy was a force for change and a great humanitarian. This book is dedicated to that force that will never die. I listen to his tapes all the time. I want to digest them and make them part of me.

In this time of instant messages and news reports being quiet is a challenge. Sitting in the UCLA archives looking for news reports given to the school by the Los Angeles Times was quiet and peaceful.

Shortly after the tragedy I sang at UCLA in an anti-war demonstration. My song was called FAITH. The beginning of that song were these words: "Jesus loves you, one and all, Mohammed will speak to you from the East, Buddah may need you those who care, and Moses will lead you only if you dare. But watch out THE DEVIL MAY TAKE YOU, OVER HOT COALS AND BAKE YOU, BUT GOD WON'T FORESAKE YOU, CAUSE HE'LL FINALLY WAKE YOU."

In keeping with the Kennedy tradition I stopped an anti-war riot in Madison, Wisconsin, Stopped the police from tear gassing students and just challenged myself to create a change in the behavior I was observing.

Wounded Knee was another challenge in which I met the leaders of the movement and did some drawings of the court trial in St. Paul, Minnesota.

Picked up former Vice-President Hubert H. Humphrey from a small airport in Winona, MN. Spent the entire day campaigning with him. The irony was not lost on me.

Gave out a thousand posters of Robert Kennedy to very happy people who put them up on their walls. They were truly beautifully done.

Went on an air base in northern California, at night, to report a hole in their fence where people could do harm to the base and got arrested, released, fed, and when asked to leave ended up getting a ride back into the base by one of the commanding officers who liked my energy and chutzpa. That night I was able to sleep on the base after running into a former classmate who received permission for me to have dinner with him. His name was Jerry Fishkes.

In my former travels around the world, at a young age, I witnessed French troops parade in Paris. They had lost the war in Vietnam. One person got shot in the face standing next to me.

WHO WERE THESE TWO HEROES, ROBERT FRANCES KENNEDY AND PRESIDENT JOHN F. KENNEDY WHO ARRIVED ON EARTH TO PREVENT A NUCLEAR WAR. THERE ARE NO ACCIDENTS. THINGS HAPPEN ON PURPOSE.

As you will find out I began painting and drawing at age seven. My first drawing was of Abraham Lincoln. I was so intense at getting his eyes right I went through the paper and had to place a paper behind it to make it look right. Lincoln looked sad.

WHAT DOES IT MEAN TO COME TO AMERICA ON A MILITARY TROOP TRANSPORT, LAND AT ELLIS ISLAND THANKSGIVING WEEK, AND FIND ONESELF ON A TRAIN TO LOS ANGELES. WE WERE DIRT POOR. GREW UP IN EAST LOS ANGELES AND LOVED TORTILLAS.

MEETING ROBERT KENNEDY AND HIS BROTHER THE PRESIDENT ARE FOREVER HIGHLIGHTS IN MY LIFE. WATCHING "ETHEL" THE DOCUMENTARY BY RORY KENNEDY WAS A GREAT MOMENT. MRS. KENNEDY WAS A POWERFUL FORCE IN THE HISTORY OF THIS NATION. I

HAVE ALSO MET KATHLEEN KENNEDY TOWNSEND, JOE KENNEDY, AND OBTAINED THE SERVICES OF PAUL ZIFFREN WHO LOVED THE KENNEDY'S.

READ, LEARN, DIGEST AND FIND OUT HOW FORTUNATE WE WERE TO LIVE IN A TIME THAT THESE GREAT HUMAN BEINGS WERE PART OF OUR LIFE.

WHEN THE CAMPAIGN ENDED THERE WAS A HOLE IN MY SOUL. I KNEW THAT I NEEDED TO REMEMBER WHAT I HAD LEARNED CAMPAIGNING FOR KENNEDY.

VISITING THE WHITE HOUSE AND ARLINGTON NATIONAL CEMETARY WAS A LONELY EXPERIENCE. I PRAYED FOR THEIR SPIRIT TO SOMEHOW GUIDE ME.

THERE IS SOME KIND OF MAGIC AT WORK SAID JOSEPH CAMPBELL AND THERE WAS LOTS OF MAGIC. AMERICA WAS YOUNG AND SHINY.

BOBBY DARIN, ONE OF MY FAVORITE SINGERS, WORKED FOR BOBBY KENNEDY IN SAN FRANCISCO SINGING AND GETTING PEOPLE OUT OUT TO VOTE. THE ENTERTAINERS FILLED THE ARENA AS KENNEY LED THE MARCH.

I RECENTLY VISITED THE R.F.K. COMMUNITY SCHOOLS BUILT ON THE SAME GROUND WHERE THE AMBASSADOR HOTEL STOOD. PAUL SCHRADE DID A GREAT JOB WITH THE LIBRARY, MURAL, AND THE SITE ITSELF. THERE WAS A PLAQUE WHERE THE STAGE WAS AND WHERE BOBBY SPOKE. WE ALSO SANG ON THAT STAGE.

SO REMEMBER CAMELOT IS OUR HERITAGE. OUR HEROES SAVED OUR LIVES AND GAVE THEIRS.

IN QUIET MOMENTS, THE AIR SO PURE, WILL FILL YOUR LIVES WITH TALES SO DEAR, THAT YOU WILL REMEMBER, THAT WE HAD THESE AMAZING HUMAN BEINGS WHO HAD NO FEAR. REMEMBER BOBBY AND JOHN. REMEMBER THEM.

HAVE FAITH.

PEACE, LEON WOLF FAINSTADT, ARTIST STILL LEARNING.

BELIEVERS AND NON BELIEVERS

I PICKED THE PRESIDENT OF THE UNITED STATES BY LOOKING AT A POSTER

Why do people pray for miracles? I believe it is because they believe in getting help from their God or the Universe. Be it Christian, Jewish, Muslim or any other religion Miracles do occur.

For no other reason than I believe that each of us has the potential for greatness. Life in itself is miraculous. Think about our planet floating in space. Yes it is floating in space and just far enough from the sun for life to exist. Now that is amazing.

I pointed to an unknown face in a poster and said: He is going to be President and then one day William Jefferson Clinton became President. I did not even know who he was or what his name was. <u>That happened and that's the truth.</u>

<u>My Grandparents, who died in Siberia, came to me in a dream.</u>

When I was 13, my grandfather and grandmother came to me in a dream. It seemed like we spent a lot of time together. My grandmother was totally quiet and never said a word. My grandfather said he was so happy to see me and said things would work out. I wondered about my grandmother not speaking to me only to find from my mother that she could not speak. They both died on that train to Siberia. My mother spoke sign language to her. My mother never told me about my grandmother not being able to speak at all. My mother was in tears as I told her about my dream. She loved her parents.

<u>BREAKING UP A RIOT IN MADISON WISCONSIN</u>

I broke up a riot in Madison, Wisconsin. I had never been there and drove about a hundred miles to see what was going on. I was campaigning for McGovern in Wisconsin and Minnesota. Not officially of course.

I arrived just in time to witness a major riot in Madison. I ended up getting arrested for giving one of the cops standing in front of the administration building the one finger salute. I ended up behind a 50 police line where that cop started chocking me. He was slammed by a highway patrol officer before he could do any more damage.

While that cop and another tried to take my picture they went through 10 rolls of polaroid film of which nothing came out. The angry cop got frantic. I remember not wanting them to have my picture. That cop finally came up to me and said: "You're doing that aren't you? Yes that was the truth don't ask me how.

COMMUNICATING WITH POLITICIANS AND HEADS OF STATE

Writing letters to heads of state and captains of industry I always believed that we are equal as human beings. Some may have more power or money but nobody can make a human being. Physically that is. We are all special.

$50,000,000 DOLLAR AD CAMPAIGN JUST BY CHANGING ONE LETTER

Once I had an idea for a major bank. I found out who to call and that bank sent out a vice president advertising to speak with me. That turned into a Fifty Million ad campaign. It ran for almost a year on television. It was like magic. Oh did I tell you that I never got paid for it. Sadly that was True.

FORETELLING THE STOCK MARKET CRASH ONE WEEK BEFORE IT HAPPENED.

A week before the 2008 Stock Market Crash, I called my brother and told him to take his money out of the position his retirement was in. We had never talked about this in the past. He eventually put his money in a low interest account. His stock went from $80.00 a share to $8.00 in one week. The market had crashed. I do not invest in the market. His saving was $500,000. Dylan Ratigan is my financial hero.

SEEING TOMORROW AND HAVING A TOW TRUCK CRASH INTO ME

I could go on and on about amazing experiences I have had and all of them I owe to my father who has been my guardian angel. Even when I was hit by a tow truck and saw it a day before it happened. It was true. I survived because I was able to see it a day before it happened in 1980. The car was destroyed.

I often wonder why I can see important events and yet cannot stop them. Not do anything about them including the assassination of Senator Robert F. Kennedy. No matter what I tried to do to protect him it was as if it did not matter. It was as if the ground kept shifting.

JETS FOR ISRAEL DURING THE KENNEDY – MCCARTHY DEBATE JUNE 1968

My singing group thought I had lost "it" and said if I spoke to anyone we would be tossed out of the campaign. I heard them, understood them, and decided I would be willing to trade my life for his if that is what it would take. As life would have it I was in the right spot at the right time and still I was asked to leave that spot and take the group downstairs. I still do not know who that person was.

I believe the Jets for Israel statement made in the debate, with McCarthy, showed that someone in his staff was not alert. It gave "them" a way to create what occurred. Gangsters, Hit Men, even Ace Security guards are in question. Thomas Noguchi, the Coroner for Los Angeles, said the fatal shot came from a distance of less than one inch. He was attacked and tossed out of his position and his character was attacked by the police. They said NO DALLAS.

SEEING THE ASSASSINATION BEFORE IT HAPPENED LIKE THE TOW TRUCK

My personal experience several nights before where I saw a gun and watched a bullet strike Bobby was horrendous for me. I thought something was wrong inside my life. I had no idea I had that ability. I was 22 years old and never paid much attention to things I could do. Once in Minneapolis I met a woman who had a photograph on her wall of a famous Indian Guru who had the ability to stop his heart and after studying the photo I told her Swami Rama was courting the girls who had joined his Yoga schools. She laughed at me but a short time later many of the women complained of his sexual advances and that small community fell apart. His "enlightened" approach was negative to say the least.

SPENDING THE DAY WITH THE FORMER VICE PRESIDENT HUBERT HUMPHREY

Spending the day with former Vice-President Humphrey was a very interesting if you take into account the fact that Robert Kennedy would have challenged him for the Presidency in 1968. Even more interesting was my waking up after an operation on my knee, barely awake, after an operation in Santa Monica and telling my wife that Hubert Humphrey had died before the medida knew. I had been sedated and asleep when I lept up and declared Hubert Humphrey died. That amazed me. Hubert H Humphrey was the one that ordered the Presidential Plane to pick up Robert Kennedy and flew him to Boston. That's the truth.

A ONE LEGGED CHICKEN SAVED MY LIFE

When my mother, father and I were in Siberia I had a one legged chicken who laid an egg-a-day. My mother said it was always on time. That one legged chicken rescued me. Siberia and labor camps were no place for a child.

I am reaching out to the nay sayers who do not recognize their own potential as miraculous human beings. Picking William Jefferson Clinton, being in touch with the Bush White House, and then connecting to the Perot Group in Texas happened just like I said. I was in touch with the major players for the Presidency and thought nothing of it. Now that is really the truth.

I have more on this but that would be too much for the person who does not believe in Miracles. My Freedom Trail Corp. was created to support education and that effort helped create a President of this country.

I used to work out at the Marriot in Century City Health Club in Los Angeles. I met former President Ronald Reagan's special Secret Service Agent. We spoke often and he said after the Robert Kennedy's assassination the Secret Service was assigned to candidates for the Presidency. He was fast on the treadmill.

THE MIDDLE EAST AND VISITORS FROM BAHRAIN AND SAUDI ARABIA

 One day I went to the dining room for lunch. I noticed a table with guests from the middle east. It was right before the first gulf war when we had former President George H. W. Bush in the white house.

I went over to their table and introduced myself and asked them what countries they were from. The were startled. One ran over to the bar just outsde the dining area and asked the bartender if I was "O.K." The bartender gave the go ahead and soon I was invited to lunch with them. The one they seemed to cater to turned out to be the son of King Abdullah of Saudi Arabia. We talked for hours about many subjects including the relationship with Jewish people. At one point he admitted he had never spoken to or met any one of the Jewish persuasion. Over a short period of time we all became comfortable with each other. We had many lunches and dinners over a two week period.

During the first war with Iraq I was invited to watch television with them. They cheered when it was announced that Iraqi planes had been shot down. You must know that it was an amazing experience. There were people in that room whose brothers shot down Iraqi jets and they were from middle eastern countries. I must say that was an amazing truth.

I know I will lose some of you that read this and maybe a lot of you. My wife keeps asking me why I am not rich. My answer is: we always have what we need.

THE FREEDOM TRAIL IS GOING TO BE REVIVED.

EDUCATION IS THE ROAD TO THE FUTURE.

SWANSTARZ AND RFK68 WILL BE SUCCESSFUL.

SEEING KNOWING ACTION

As an artist I am able to see things three dimensionally. I know this is a lot to take in but it is for the good of the planet. I once replayed an entire horse race after it was done. It was like rewinding a tape. I could see three dimensionally.

FROM GROWING UP SHY TO SINGING ON STAGE

As a singer I have performed for thousands of people and on one occasion 50,000 people at UCLA. Our group THE SOUNDS OF TIME was created by opening a large phone book, closing my eyes, and putting my finger on a name

having that person be a talented singer. Gayleen Woodruff and Jim Wolk were great. We worked well together. I did all the talking on stage.

AFTER KENNEDY DIED

I have never told anyone this but after Robert Kennedy died I climbed the largest pine tree in the back yard. I held on to the top branch and allowed my body to literally swing from that branch. I thought about dying. I was sad that I saw what was coming and was not able to prevent it. I blamed myself. Jim and Gayleen asked me to come down but I just hung there transfixed by how beautiful the sky looked. That sky saved me. I realized how amazing our lives were. I climbed back down. I would become one of Robert Kennedy's Ripples of Hope. It has taken me 46 years to finally break through.

ROSEMARY CLOONEY SUFFERED GREATLY AFTER RFK DIED

I loved dancing with Rosemary Clooney and she was having a great time. She had a bunch of nice kids with her that danced on the floor. The press loved it. She was very sad when Bobby was killed. We all fell apart. She had a great smile.

THE SOUNDS OF TIME ON THE FRONT PAGE OF THE L.A.TIMES ON JUNE 5, 1968

On June 5, 1968 THE SOUNDS OF TIME were on the front page of the Los

Angeles Time with a sad headline SEN. KENNEDY SHOT AT VICTORY FETE.

It was my birthday and that newspaper showed how prescient my father had been as he laid in a hospital bed being prepped for a brain tumor operation. In 1950 brain opertions were rarely successful. He died but not before telling me that my life would be bitter-sweet and I needed to enjoy both. He smiled and showed me how to be courageous.

WE STILL LIVE IN INTERESTING TIMES

Once a great President Kennedy said WE LIVE IN INTERESTING TIMES.

Well I agree. President John F. Kennedy and his brother Robert F. Kennedy saved the world and the human race from being involved in a nuclear war with Russia. They stood up to the most powerful military machine, ours, and pushed them back from the brink of war. Love them forever. Pray that this generation of politicians have the courage to make peace. Women will step forward.

WOMEN ARE THE PRAYER FULLFILLED AND THE ANSWER

Over SIX BILLION people on this planet and only three billion of tha six make most of the decisions. Isn't it time for a change? I vote for women to help make a difference and fight for peace. Operating on half of our cylinders is a losing proposition. THE TIMES THEY ARE A CHAINGIN. Bob Dylan said that.

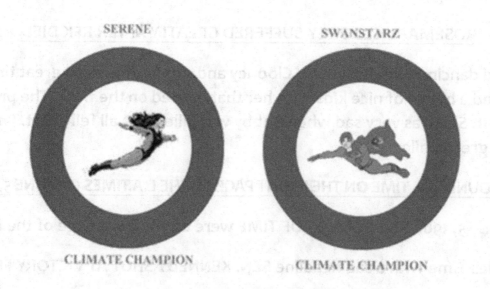

SERENE   SWANSTARZ

CLIMATE CHAMPION   CLIMATE CHAMPION

THE SWANSTARZ SISTER AND BROTHER TEAM FROM THE MILKY WAY

TO HELP CHILDREN WHO SUFFERED FROM BREATHING POLLUTED AIR.

Swanstarz, the idea, came out of a very fast drawing. I drew a husband, wife, and a child. The major impact of a child with wings and swans feet stopped me cold. I studied that painting and then spent seven years studying swans, our planet, climate change, and ultimately why human beings have a tendency to destroy each other. In this situation Climate Change would be a war that nobody could win. That quick drawing turned into a website: Swanstarz.com,

Communication with countries in Europe regarding the catastrophic effects of climate change and how it will cause a new kind of war around the globe. There will be wars over water and food. You will not want to be there.

I met former Vice-President Al Gore in Burbank. The airplane hanger was at least 115 degrees in the shade. Al Gore has gone on to do more than he ever could have done as President. I believe he is creating the conditions for people to wake up to the reality of our planet.

SWANSTARZ, the future film, will allow even those who harm the planet to wake up. That is a tall order. Salt Talks, on climate change, will move us forward.

SWANSTARZ.COM

HE WILL LOVE SWANSTARZ

I LOVE THE SMILE ON HIS FACE

MY HERO

Germany-1947

Mendel/Leon Fajnstadt

PHOTO TAKEN IN GERMANY IN 1947

THE NEXT PAGE IS THAT FIRST SWANSTARZ FAMILY

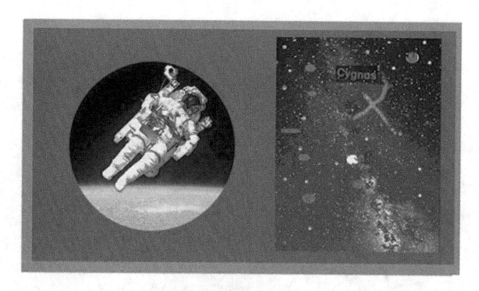

ARIEL PRAYED FOR ALL THE CHILDREN OF THE EARTH

A CHILD'S PRAYER BRINGS SALVATION FOR OUR PLANET EARTH. ARIEL, ATTACHED TO AN OXYGEN TANK, PRAYS FOR ALL CHILDREN. HER PRAYERS BRING SWANSTARZ TO TEACH THOSE WITHOUT UNDERSTANDING THE HARM THEIR MACHINERY WILL DO TO FUTURE GENERATIONS.

WHAT DOES ALL THIS HAVE TO DO WITH ROBERT F. KENNEDY? **EVERYTHING.** OUR KENNEDY AND YOUR KENNEDY WAS ABOUT SELFLESS ACTIONS AND SERVICE TO COUNTRY. IN SO DOING HE SERVED HUMANITY.

WHAT ARE THOSE RIPPLES OF HOPE IF NOT THE ACTIONS WE TAKE DAILY. WE ARE THE RIPPLES OF HOPE THAT EACH OF US CAN CREATE? THEY ARE AN AVALANCHE OF LOVE AND CARING AND YOU NAME IT. THAT'S A RIPPLE.

IN THE COMING MONTHS ART FILM FASHION WILL LAUNCH AN ALL-OUT-WAR ON STUPIDITY AND HUBRIS. WHAT "THEY" DON'T KNOW WILL HURT FUTURE GENERATIONS OF THEIR OFFSPRINGS OFFSPRING.

WHAT'S LOVE GOT TO DO WITH IT? EVERYTHING.

I AM LEARNING A LOT ABOUT THOMAS MERTON AND HAVE LEARNED A LOT ABOUT BUDDHISM OVER THE YEARS AND HAVE FOUND THAT MOST PEOPLE JUST WANT TRUTH.HOW ABOUT SOME.

PEACE. LEON W. FAINSTADT

WE CAME TO AMERICA LIKE MILLIONS BEFORE US

Who would believe that 12 years later I would meet a most amazing person. President Kennedy at the beach in Santa Monica. We were racing towards the moon and the future of mankind.

My mother became a radio and television star and a member of SAG. Johnny Carson, late television talk show host, loved her.

HEY LET'S MAKE A MOVIE

THE NEXT TIME YOU HEAR NUCLEAR

REMEMBER HOW MUCH THEY
GAVE TO OUR COUNTRY

BLESSINGS.

THE
BEGINNING
R.F.K. '68

LION WOLF
FAINSTADT

I CAME TO AMERICA WHEN I WAS 5 YEARS OLD FROM PARIS, FRANCE AFTER THE DEATH OF MY FATHER AT AGE 39. I SPOKE FRENCH AND YIDDISH. MY FIRST DRAWING AS AN ARTIST WAS OF ABRAHAM LINCOLN WHEN I WAS SEVEN,

ALTHOUGH I COULD NOT SPEAK, OR READ ENGLISH, I COULD FEEL HIS GAZE FROM A PHOTO, THAT LOOK IN HIS EYES CAPTURED MY HEART AND ATTENTION. I COULD "FEEL" LINCOLN. I LATER WOULD LEARN WHAT A GREAT MAN HE WAS. HIS EYES LOOKED SAD JUST LIKE THE AMERICAN SOLDIERS WE SAT ACROSS FROM IN THE TRUCKS. WE RACED ACROSS EUROPE. AMERICAN SOLDIERS WERE SAVIORS.

WHEN JACK SMITH ASKED ME WHY I LIKED SEN. KENNEDY AND I TOLD HIM THAT HE RIMINDED ME OF ABRAHAM LINCOLN. HE LOOKED SURPRISED BUT I FELT THE COMPASSION IN LINCOLN'S EYES.

LINCOLN, JFK, RFK, MLK, AND A FEW OTHERS WOULD HAVE HAD A GREAT CONVERSATION. PERHAPS THEY STILL ARE TALKING TO EACH OTHER ON A LEVEL WE DO NOT UNDERSTAND.

TRUST ME THERE ARE THINGS WE DON'T KNOW.

I SENSE DANGER. I AM UNCOMFORTABLE.

I KNOW THEY ARE COMING!

We're on stage. I'm looking out at the crowd and searching the faces intensely. **What will he, she, or they, look like.** I have never looked for a killer before but I must keep looking. Suddenly I see someone that looks distracted while we are singing. Jumping off the stage I land hard on the floor and I am in someone's face. I put the microphone in front of their face and ask them to sing. They look startled as I search their eyes for fear. I am looking for any reason to stop them before they act. I continue this search.

Soon I am dancing with several kids and **Rosemary Clooney** who is all smiles. The cameras' from NBC, ABC, and Canada are now focused on the crowd in front of the stage as we are singing "This man is your man, this man is my man, from California to the New York Islands." And all the time we sing and smile. For a moment I am just another person in the Embassy Ballroom and not someone ready to give their life for Bobby. I jump back onstage after dancing with another woman who has to be at least 80 years old but who is dancing right along with everyone. The crowd loves her.

Hey! sing with me! I call out to someone in the crowd. Someone who does not fit. How will I know them? It does not matter. Soon we are done with our set on stage and we take a break. I am preparing for anything to come our way.

The pantry and kitchen behind the stage.

This guard is tall and wearing a uniform and has a gun strapped to his hip. He is all smiles as I confront him again and again.

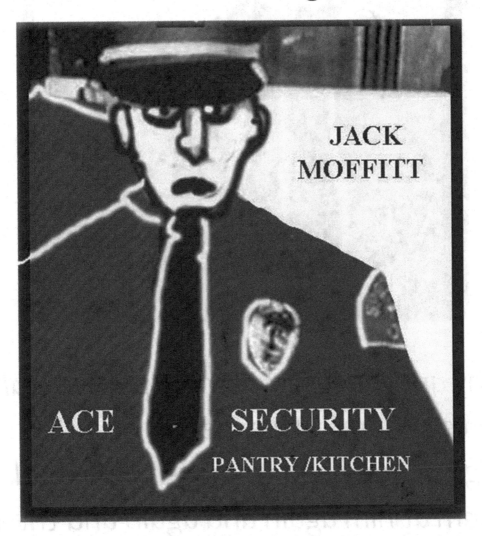

I did not let up chastising him all night.

I later learn that the hotel hired ACE.

JACK
MOFFITT

ACE   ·   SECURITY
PANTRY /KITCHEN

"Why are you just watching people walk into this room?" They need a security badge or you need to move them out I scream at him again and again and then he finally breaks and starts to get mad at me.

Jack: "If you don't stop I am going to just have to clobber you." He says. I do not back down and continue to berate him for his lack of professionalism. He is too busy watching he girls go by. He is not doing his job at all.

"If someone does not have a security badge! Just ask them to leave!" I continue to berate him <u>then turn to push people out of the area. Most of those in the room have no badges.</u>

I move to the Colonial Room and see Milton Berle. I yell Milton Berle! And he jumps up, looks around, and yells back **WHERE**? I laugh and tell him I can't top that. He smiles. I turn to go back into the pantry.

Time seems compressed. I am preparing myself to intervene. To stop anyone that looks like a threat. I am totally prepared mentally to give my life if I have to. I cried like a baby when John Kennedy died. I met him in Santa Monica when I was 17 and was not going to let anyone hurt his brother.

My father's death at 39, in Paris, had created a young person who was fearless. I had prepared myself to become unafraid of anything including death. I was ready

for anything. When I came to America
I even went to far as to see how long
I could hold my arm under hot water,
pinch, punch, you name it I wanted to be
fearless.

WE WERE BACK ON STAGE

Jim is singing: "You see this guy, this guys in love with you" a beautiful song by Herb Alpert another Fairfax High graduate. He lived a couple blocks from me.

Jim was singing his heart out. We moved people with our music and energy.

C'mon I yelled as I lept off the stage time and time again. Looking for eyes that were fearfull or nervous. Anything that would give someone away.

Then I was dancing with Rosemary again and the floor seemed to open up and circled around us. It was amazing and we were all smiling. Bobby was winning. Rosemary Clooney was so very happy then.

The crowd erupted again into: WE WANT BOBBY! WE WANT BOBBY! THEY CALLED OUT TO BRING HIM DOWN TO US.

PRE JUNE 5, 1968 THE SADDEST DAY

It was getting closer to midnight and my birthday, June 5th, and someone said he was coming. I went around to the side of the stage, through a curtain, and waited for him to clear the kitchen, pantry, and get him on stage. Then he was there. Smiling.

He walked up to me and shook my hand to thank us for working on his behalf and smiled. I was all smiles and said: "Thank You Mr. President. **I'll see you in the white house!** He walked by, turned, and smiled to say thanks again and turned back to go through the curtain and climb onto the stage. California was in the victory column.

I would stay behind. Jim and Gayleen were onstage with him but I was comfortable to stay behind the curtain and protect the rear of the stage and block anyone from going through that curtain. I was a sentry.

Someone tapped my shoulder.

I did not know who this man was but he told me to get the group and go downstairs to an overflow crowd. **He said**

Kennedy would soon join me. I resisted. I told him I was not going anywhere. He insisted and I noticed a security button on his lapel. I still insisted on staying exactly where I was. He kept pushing and said please leave, go get your group, and he will be with you in a minute. I PROMISE he said. Really? Yes Yes I <u>PROMISE</u> he will soon be with you. People have been waiting downstairs for hours.

IT WAS A SHORT WALK DOWN THE STAIRS WHICH LED TO A SMALL STAGE.

I TURNED, OPENED THE CURTAIN, SAW BOBBY WITH MY GROUP ON STAGE AND ASKED THEM TO FOLLOW ME.

"HE WILL BE WITH US SHORTLY" JIM AND GAYLEEN FOLLOWED ME DOWN THE STAIRS. THEY LOOKED SURPRISED.

<u>LESS THAN 20 SECONDS</u>

IT TOOK US LESS THAN 20 SECONDS TO GO DOWN THE STAIRS. I WAS VERY UPSET. I STEPPED ON STAGE, TOOK ONE LOOK AT THE CROWD, WHO SUDDENLY LOOKED ANIMATED, AND REALIZED THAT IT WAS TOO LATE AND TURNED TO JIM AND GAYLEEN AND SAID: **SEE! THEY HAVE KILLED HIM!** I THEN I BEGAN TO RUN BACK TOWARDS THE STAIRS WHICH ALREADY HAD BEEN BLOCKED BY THE LOS ANGELES POLICE DEPARTMENT. THEY WOULD NOT LET ME GO BACK UP. I WAS FRANTIC.

I RACED THROUGH A DOOR THAT LED TO A STAIRWAY DOWN TO THE PARKING LOT BELOW. I HIT THE PARKING LOT AND RAN FAST. MY HEART WAS RACING AS I RAN THROUGH THE CARS AND WATCHED A POLICEMAN LOWER HIS MOTORCYCLE, WITH HIS GUN DRAWN, AS HE BEGAN RUNNING TOWARDS THE HOTEL. **<u>DAMN! DAMN! DAMN!</u>** I HURTLED TOWARDS THE ENTRANCE AND THROUGH THE CROWD THAT HAD PEOPLE IN TEARS AND RAN BACK AROUND TO THE BALLROOM ENTRANCE. I WAS LOOKING FOR THE ACE GUARD. JACK WAS RIGHT THERE.

I RAN UP TO HIM AND BEGAN SCREAMING: **I TOLD YOU HE WOULD GET HURT!**

HE LOOKED AT ME CALMLY, AS HE STOOD TO GUARD THE KITCHEN ENTRANCE, AND TOLD ME: DON'T WORRY.

<u>"He is going to be O.K.! He was only grazed by a bullet in his leg!"</u>

<u>Are you sure I screamed at him and he repeated: He was only grazed in the leg. He is going to be fine.</u>

<u>He had lied to me</u> and his lie made me turn away from the calamity that I could hear in the kitchen and the crowd as I turned to comfort people who were hysterically crying in the ballroom. I believed him until I went back to our hotel room and turned on the television.

Gabor Kadar, a friend, was being interviewed by a news station. He was incoherent and crying at the same time and talked about a little man who had pulled a gun out next to him and who had begun to scream at Kennedy while pulling the trigger.

Gabor can be heard in many documentaries and news clips screaming:

GET THE GUN! GET THE GUN!, BREAK HIS HAND. AND THEN POINTING TO HIS OWN HEAD AND MAKING A MOTION TO SAY THAT BOBBY HAD BEEN SHOT IN THE HEAD.

NOW I BEGAN TO CRY HYSTERICALLY.

GABOR KADAR HAD BEEN STANDING NEXT TO SIRHAN WHO WAS STANDING OPPOSITE WHERE I WOULD HAVE BEEN HAD I NOT BEEN ASKED TO MOVE OUR SINGING GROUP DOWNSTAIRS.

I HAD FIGURED OUT THE EXACT PLACE TO STAND TO PROTECT ROBERT KENNEDY.

GABOR DID NOT HAVE A TICKET SO HE
SNUCK INTO THE KITCHEN IN THE HOPES
HE COULD HEAR US SING. HE WALKED
INTO HELL. HE SPOKE AND THEN CRIED.

My STATUEOF LIBERTY WAS IN TEARS.

**HE WAS ALL ALONE. HARD
EDGES NO EXIT.**

I STILL PRAY FOR HIM EVERY DAY.

A friend, Dr. Jayson Sher, took photos after people left the ballroom and saved them in an airtight special box he designed. He allowed me to use them for this book. This crumpled Kennedy sign, found in the ballroom, says a lot about that night. Dr. Sher and his father were photographers who often took pictures of weddings and parties at the Ambassador hotel for years. He had not opened this box until I told him about this book. He had kept it unopened for 46 years. He was my doctor.

THE ACE SECURITY GUARDS. THE TALL ONE
IS THE ONE I YELLED AT ALL NIGHT. THANE
EUGENE CESAR WAS THE ACE GUARD WHO
WAS BEHIND BOBBY.

CESAR WAS THE ONE NEAR KENNEDY WHEN HE WAS SHOT.

CESAR WAS THE "SO CALLED PROTECTION" FOR
KENNEDY WHEN HE CAME DOWN FROM HIS ROOM TO
ADDRESS THE CROWD. ALL THE ACE SECURITY GUARDS
FAILED AT PROTECTING ROBERT KENNEDY.

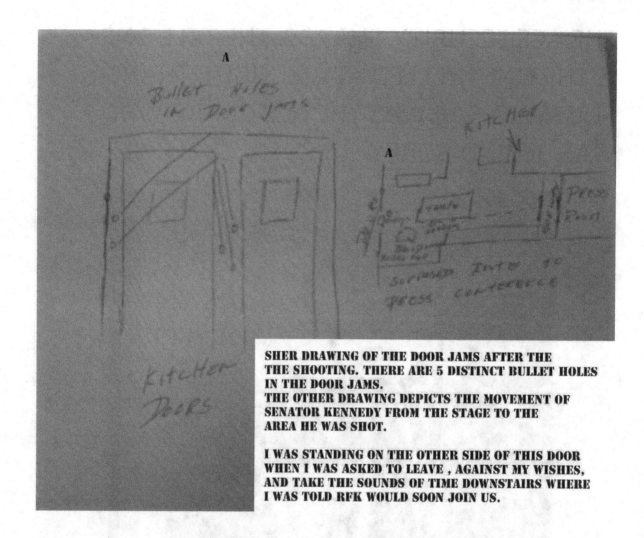

SHER DRAWING OF THE DOOR JAMS AFTER THE
THE SHOOTING. THERE ARE 5 DISTINCT BULLET HOLES
IN THE DOOR JAMS.
THE OTHER DRAWING DEPICTS THE MOVEMENT OF
SENATOR KENNEDY FROM THE STAGE TO THE
AREA HE WAS SHOT.

I WAS STANDING ON THE OTHER SIDE OF THIS DOOR
WHEN I WAS ASKED TO LEAVE , AGAINST MY WISHES,
AND TAKE THE SOUNDS OF TIME DOWNSTAIRS WHERE
I WAS TOLD RFK WOULD SOON JOIN US.

SCHEMATIC OF THE EMBASSY ROOM AND KITCHEN AREA.

THIS WAS A DRAWING DR. SHER MADE IMMEDIATELY
AFTER THE ASSASSINATION. HE COUNTED THE BULLET
HOLES.

June 5, 1968

MY BIRTHDAY

I am listening to Robert Kennedy speak but I am in back of the curtain. I want to protect his back. My group is on stage with Kennedy and are all smiles. I am happy where I am.

My stomach is turning and I am very nervous still. This is the vulnerable area. I am certain.

The curtain seperates the stage from the swinging doors that lead to the kitchen. It is here that I have decided that my Kennedy is the most vulnerable. Yes your Kennedy.

The Ace Security guards and I have not been getting along all night as they are still not doing their jobs. I have an awful feeling that something is going to happen and believe that there are no safe exits on this night for our candidate. I learn that Pierre Salinger told him to stay out of the kitchen. He thought there were too many hard and sharp edges.

In between our entertaining the crowd and looking for an assassin I am back in front of the guard. In his face again.

June 5, is my 23rd birthday, and its been only a year since the Six Day War. Being

Jewish that is a day that was burned into my psyche.

Dammit the guard is spending more time looking at the girls than doing his job.

I begin to kick people out again. I clear the kitchen again and again. If I do not see a ticket I force people back into the ballroom.

I am in his face again as he threaten me with violence if

I keep harassing him. Ace is not much of an Ace.

The tallest guard Jack Moffitt is the one who has threatened me and he knows I am on his case. I am not letting up on his lax attitude. He is full of himself.

You had to be there. Their uniform made them look real but they were not. I turned and began throwing people out. People were getting angry with me but no clearance and they were thrown back out into the embassy ballroom.

SECOND INTRODUCTION

AND OPENING

I am writing this book because I cannot figure out how to draw it.

R.F.K.'68

INSIDE THE LAST CAMPAIGN

THE AMBASSADOR HOTEL

LEON WOLF FAINSTADT

"THE SOUNDS OF TIME"

THE ENTERTAINMENT GROUP FOR R.F.K.

SPECIAL THANKS TO:

To my family and friends

Janet, my wife, and Rachele, my daughter

who begged me to write this story. They heard it a hundred times.

To my parents who endured the Nazi onslaught in Poland only to be put in a Soviet Gulag Slave Camp for six years from 1939 to 1945.

For the Six Million and Millions of others who perished.

SHALOM - PEACE

Dr. Jayson I. Sher who took photographs after the assassination and kept them in a sealed container, unopened, for 46 years. Many of his photographs are contained in this book. He was very generous to let me use them.

To the Senator Robert F. Kennedy family who continue creating value for America and the world. Especially to Mrs. Ethel Kennedy and Jerry Bruno who picked my group, "The Sounds of Time", to be the advance singing group for southern California.

To President John F. Kennedy who I met in Santa Monica two months before the Cuban Missile Criisis in October 1962 when I was 17 years old. His first handshake was not strong so I ran after him into the pacific ocean and asked him for a second one. He was surprised and then laughed. His second one was strong. I realized, later, that people squeezed too hard so they just wanted to touch and go. I learned with the R.F.K. campaign.

To the hundreds of millions of people that President John F. Kennedy and Senator Robert F. Kennedy saved by preventing a nuclear war with the Soviet Union. To the extended families who owe their lives to the courageous actions of two amazing human beings. We owe them so much.

To Vasily Arkhipov, of the Soviet Union, who did not fire his nuclear missiles as his submarine came under attack by American warships. His courage, along with the Kennedy's prevented a catastrophic nuclear war in 1962

CONTENTS

Being an artist this book is organized in a sequence of words and images that tell my story. Unlike the standard book, with pages and a narrative, this book is designed so the reader can understand what I experienced while working with the Robert F. Kennedy Presidential Campaign in Southern California.

<u>There are some experiences I had that will be hard to believe but they are true.</u> Some may have qualified for the twilight zone. Keep reading and you will understand. I was born the day World War II was officially declared over by the Generals from America, Russia, England, and France. That would be June 5, 1945. They stood proudly having defeated a devil of a man. I was very lucky.

The Generals were Eisenhower

Who delayed D-day from the 5th of June to the 6th of June.

Montgomery of England

Zhukov of The Soviet Union and

DeGaulle of France

On September 1, 1939 my mother watched the Luftwaffe fly, in formation, over her home in Poland. The family consisted of my grandfather Wolf Leib, Sheindle, grandmother, My uncles Moshe and David Walker. Theirs was a simple existence until that day. The family consisted of tailors who made leather pants and jackets.

Rose, my mother, watched as the planes began to bomb Poland. My father, to be, was in the Polish cavalry and fought courageously, survived, and was sent to the gulags in Siberia. Berl Fajerberg would one day become my step-father and fought in the trenches. He was shot five times. Once in both arms, his chest, and once in the throat just missing his windpipe and was captured by the German army. He never spoke about the war that killed his entire family. He just showed my brother Jack and I his bullet wounds and shook his head.

HITLER AND HIS STAFF / WHAT UGLY HUMAN BEINGS THEY WERE

STALIN, IN CONCERT WITH HITLER, HAD A TRUCE. THAT ALLOWED MY PARENTS TO ESCAPE POLAND. THEY WENT FROM THE FRYING PAN INTO THE FIRE AND WERE SENT TO THE GULAG IN SIBERIA FOR SIX YEARS – 1939-1945.

HITLER AND STALIN CAUSED THE DEATHS OF OVER 60 MILLION PEOPLE

MY PARENTS WERE FORTUNATE TO SURVIVE

THE RUSSIANS WELCOMED US ONTO CATTLE CARS FOR SLAVE LABOR IN SIBERIA. I WOULD NOT BE WRITING THIS BOOK WITHOUT THAT AGREEMENT.

THE WEATHER WAS -50 DEGREES.

AMAZING HOW PATHS CROSS EACH OTHER LIKE THOSE RIPPLES OF
HOPE THAT ROBERT KENNEDY HAS INSCRIBED IN ARLINGTON, VIRGINA

THOSE RIPPLES OF HOPE ARE THE FUTURE OF OUR WORLD.

JEWS WERE BEING PUT INTO CATTLE CARS ON THE WAY TO THE GULAGS

LIKE THIS TRANSPORT. NOTHING TO SUSTAIN THEM EXCEPT FAITH.

IT WAS EITHER THE GULAGS OR THE CREMATORIUMS

EITHER WAY THE CATTLE CARS WERE DEATH
SENTENCES FOR MANY MILLIONS

OF JEWS WHO COULD NOT BELIEVE THIS WOULD EVER HAPPEN.

My Grandparents died on that train to Siberia and
were buried somewhere in the forests. It is hard to
explain and imagine what people suffered.

On the way to the trains my parents and her family had to
cross over a bridge from Poland to Russia and my mother
saw the German soldiers under the bridge. She felt that
the soldiers were going to blow up the bridge.

They were able to cross because both Germany and
Russia were not prepared to do battle so the "truce"
was a way to buy time. The worst was coming.

SEEING TOMORROW IS OFTEN PAINFUL

I am sitting with Senator Kennedy and Mrs. Ethel Kennedy, Jim Wolk and Gayleen Woodruff. We have just finished entertaining a large crowd in the garden. Robert Kennedy is to my left and Mrs. Kennedy is next to him opposite me. I suddenly feel that someone is behind me, almost touching my back, and then I feel a hand and then an arm extend over my right shoulder.

I see a gun barrel and then a bullet, that is moving in slow motion, I can even see the revolution of the bullet as I watch it strike Robert Kennedy's head.

I drop my head and cannot believe what I just experienced. When I lift my head back up I must have a look of concern as Ethel Kennedy notices my discomfort. She continues to look at me and then I begin to get some color back in my face.

What was that? Why did that happen to me. Everything is fine as the crowd is listening with rapt attention to Bobby as he talks about what he wants to accomplish as President. The crowd continues to ask him about his brother which must be very painful. They want the truth and he continues to tell them, as always, that he must become President in order for the truth to come out. He has to be on the inside. Truth is difficult to find.

I am quite distraught as that experience continues to play in my head. <u>Am I sick?</u> I question myself in silence. Why did I see those things. One day I will find out. That has shaken me along with my fear of June 5th.

<u>I remember something about the Trojan wars.</u>

Cassandra

Cassandra was able to foretell events in the future. This caused her to be ridiculed. At one point she ran towards the Trojan horse and tried to burn the straw horse but was stopped by her own people. They saw the horse as a gift. The enemies of Greece were inside that horse. Greece would fall. Cassandra was in constant pain over this.

She continued to see events of the future and was never taken seriously.

My singing group heard my words of fear about the pending June 5th date and the previous Arab-Israeli War of 1967. They watched the same debate I did but could never have understood what I was talking about and feared what my words would cause our group. I had to find another way.

The Greeks are still losing.

My singing group thought I had gone over the edge when I warned them that Senator Kennedy was in grave danger.He had promised to send 50 Phantom Jets to Israel one week before the anniversary of the Six Day War.

I was screaming at the television that those words would be used to kill him. I am sure that sounded crazy to anyone who heard me.

<u>Sirhan heard the same thing I did.</u>

How? I knew the history of that date. There is something in survivors of the holocaust that enables a certain ability to see things that others will never see. It's a vision thing. I realized that anyone who heard me would think something was wrong with me. <u>I made up my mind to protect him myself.</u>

MANY PEOPLE TOOK PICTURES
OF ME WITH SEN. KENNEDY. THEY
TRIED TO GIVE THEM TO ME BUT
I HAD NOWHERE TO KEEP THEM.
YEARS LATER I TOLD JOE ABOUT
MY EXPERIENCE AND THIS WAS
THE RESULT.NICE PHOTO.

PHOTO TAKEN AT THE JFK LIBRARY IN BOSTON

MY TEARS FLOWED LIKE A RIVER AT THE JFK LIBRARY

I WAS WITH THE FAMILY BUT COULD SAY NOTHING.

WHAT THE KENNEDY BROTHERS

DID FOR AMERICA AND THE WORLD.

THE KENNEDY BROTHERS

SAVED US ALL

AMERICA WOULD HAVE LOST

100 MILLION PEOPLE IN 15 MINUTES

THE KENNEDY BROTHERS FOUGHT OFF THE MILITARY WHO WANTED TO GO INTO CUBA. THEY DID NOT KNOW THAT THERE WERE NUCLEAR TIPPED MISSLES PREPARED TO LAUNCH AND THE CONFLAGRATION WAS ON.

THEY HAD THE COURAGE TO LOOK FOR PEACE.

Neil Sheehan is a great writer. I first saw him interviewed on Charley Rose. He was talking about many things and then suddenly began to praise the Kennedy brothers for saving the lives of millions of Americans. There is no other family that has given so much to the United States. "He saved us!"

COURAGE RAN THROUGH THEIR VEINS.

I started to think about those hundred million and realize that over time that would grow to so many it would be hard to count. Many of us alive today owe our existence to President Kennedy and Robert Kennedy. I pray for them every single day. Both brothers are forever in my heart.

THEY SAVED US ALL.

REMEMBER THEM WELL AMERICA.

James Douglass, a friend, wrote

"JFK and the UNSPEAKABLE"

If you want to know the truth look no further about JFK's *move towards peace* than this book.

I first heard about him while watching
Charley Rose interviewing Oliver Stone.
Oliver Stone picked up the book and

waved it in the air.

He said it was the best book ever about JFK
and his assassination. I could only read three
pages at a time. The book is that powerful.
The words were like daggers. James Douglass
wrote the book longhand. Look for his books.

He is a quiet giant whose words
penetrate the heart. I was fortunate to be
interviewed by James for three hours.

He exudes Integrity. He is a man of faith. Our
interview led me to know of Thomas Merton.
Thomas Merton was an amazing human being.

THREE WHO SAVED US

President Kennedy, Robert F. Kennedy and Vasili Arkhipov

Vasili was in a submarine off the coast of Cuba
when his submarine came under attack by an
American Warship. The apparent reason was the
communications were down and most on the sub
thought we were already in a nuclear war.

The Commander ordered Vasili Arkhipov

to launch his nuclear missiles.

He refused to believe there was a nuclear war
between The Soviet Union and America.

Had Vasili launched his missiles, as
ordered, the world would

Have become a burnt cinder and as President Kennedy so

aptly put it in his last major speech at American University
that we would all end up with ashes in our mouths.

THERE IS NO VICTORY THAT IS NUCLEAR

THE FRONT PAGE

Of the L.A.Times

ON JUNE 5, 1968

IMPORTANT PHOTO

SINCE NOBODY SEEMS TO HAVE SEEN IT

The Sounds of Time at the Ambassador Hotel's Embassy Room.

I am the one ready to unfold a peace sign. By the time this book is published it should be on display in bookstores across America.

Next to the ABC cameraman. Kris Desautel is next to me and Jim Wolk is standing on the far right holding his guitar. "we want Bobby" is loud and clear in the room.

Peace Signs are visible throughout the room.

IN YIDDISH THE WORD BASHERT MEANS MEANT TO BE

BOBBY KENNEDY AT AGE 22 WAS IN
JERUSALEM ON JUNE 5, 1948

My third birthday was in Paris, France on June 5, 1948

I BEGAN WORKING WITH SEN. KENNEDY WHEN I WAS
22 YEARS OLD AND WOULD TURN 23 ON JUNE 5, 1968

I WAS BORN IN A SLAVE LABOR CAMP IN
A COUNTRY CALLED KAZAKHSTAN. THE
SOVIETS KNEW IT AS SIBERIA.

BOBBY KENNEDY VISITED KAZAKHSTAN WITH
JUSTICE DOUGLAS AFTER WORLD WAR II.

THAT GULAG/CAMP WAS LESS THEN 500 MILES
FROM SEMIPATALANSK WHERE THE SOVIETS
EXPLODED NUCLEAR WEAPONS AFTER THE END
OF THE SECOND WORLD WAR. THEY EXPLODED

HUNDREDS OF THEM AND ENDED UP DESTROYING
THE LIVES OF MANY SOVIET CITIZENS.

<u>THE TRACES OF THAT POISON DISFIGURES KIDS TODAY.</u>

KAZAKHSTAN ASKED THE SOVIET UNION
TO TAKE BACK THE NUCLEAR MISSILES
THEY HAD ON KAZAKH TERRITORY.

TED TURNER HELPED THE UNITED STATES IN THE EFFORT

TO LESSEN A NUCLEAR THREAT.

HE IS A VISIONARY. A GREAT MAN. APPRECIATE HIM!

THE KAZAKH PEOPLE ARE PRIMARILY
MONGOLIAN IN ORIGIN.

THE PLACE I WAS BORN IS SIXTY MILES FROM CHINA.

THERE ARE A LOT OF STANS AND
KAZAKHSTAN IS A COUNTRY THAT VALUES
THEIR PEOPLE AND FREEDOM. BRAVO.

THE CAMPS/75% OF THOSE WHO ENTERED PERISHED.

THE DEBATE

JUNE 1, 1968

McCARTHY VS. KENNEDY

KENNEDY: "WHEN I AM PRESIDENT I WILL SEND 50 PHANTOM JETS TO ISRAEL"

THE JUNE 5, 1967

ARAB-ISRAELI WAR ONE YEAR BEFORE.

I HEARD THOSE WORDS ON THE TELEVISED

DEBATE AND KNEW HE WAS IN TROUBLE.

THE ANNIVERSARY WAS PRIMARY DAY

I WAS STARTLED AND SCREAMED THEY WILL USE THAT TO KILL HIM. MY MEMBERS BEGGED ME TO KEEP QUIET. WORDS ARE DANGEROUS.

FOR ISRAEL

MY GROUP WAS AFRAID WE'D BE ASKED TO LEAVE THE CAMPAIGN. I MADE UP MY MIND TO PROTECT HIM.

MY FATHER TAUGHT ME ABOUT COURAGE WHEN HE WAS DYING AT THE AGE OF 39 IN PARIS FRANCE. HE HAD A BRAIN TUMOR. HE NEVER STOPPED SMILING.

MY FATHER'S SPIRIT WAS WITH ME ALWAYS.

Kennedy: "Jets for Israel" statement

LEON: "SOMEONE JUST HEARD THAT AND THEY WILL USE THAT TO KILL HIM."

THE CAMPAIGN IS OVER!!!."

JIM AND GAYLEEN MADE ME PROMISE NOT TO SAY ANYTHING. THEY PLEADED WITH ME.

THEY SAID OUR GROUP WILL BE KICKED OUT OF THE CAMPAIGN AND NOBODY WOULD BELIEVE ME ANYWAY.

SEEING THE FUTURE IS

A LONELY BUSINESS.

JUST ASK CASSANDRA.

MY BIRTHDAY WAS COMING UP ON JUNE 5, 1968. IT IS THE ONE YEAR ANNIVERSARY OF THE ARAB-ISRAELI WAR. PRIMARY DAY IN CALIFORNIA. I CANNOT RELAX.

My mind begins to race. What can I do. I am determined to stop any threat with my own life if necessary. My father's death has prepared me to be fearless.

"I AM AT THE LION'S GATE IN MY MIND"

ENTERING THE OLD CITY

SIX MILLION PEOPLE ARE
ON BOTH SIDES OF ME.

THE DEAD ARE REBORN AND WITH ME.

LION WOLF

FAINSTADT

THE NAME IS NOT AN ACCIDENT

Defense Minister Moshe Dayan, Chief of Staff Yitzhak Rabin and Jerusalem Commander Uzinarkis enter through Lion's gate into the Old City. -GPO 06/07/1967

SIX DAYS AND IT WAS OVER (FOR A WHILE)

Israeli paratroopers stood in front of the Western Wall in Jerusalem. -GPO 06/07/1967

My birthday, June 5, 1967, was very difficult for me as my heritage was Jewish. Our family had suffered greatly in the second world war thus the connection was deep. The Only reason my mother, brother, and I were not in Isreal was due to the fact that my mother's only remaining brother David Walker threatened to never talk to her again if she brought her sons to Israel. The inner fear about the looming birthday was making my determination even stronger. I would give my life for his. I would spend the remaining days looking for any threat. That unusual experience on that stage earlier in the week was very hard for me. I HAD NEVER EXPERIENCED SOMETHING SO STARK.

PRIMARY DAY

IN CALIFORNIA

JUNE 4, 1968

PRIMARY DAY IN CALIFORNIA JUNE 4, 1968

Everyone looks happy and nervous at the same time. Robert Kennedy has done all he can to gain victory in California. Gayleen, Jim, and myself are given instructions to keep the place jumping with music and to create enthusiasm like cheer leaders. I am ready but extremely concerned. The vision I had is haunting me. Why did I have it? I see that bullet in slow motion. Will I be ready to give my life for his? I am not afraid. The evening is upon us. It is primary day in California. I will shield him.

The Ambassador was a historic hotel and quite beautiful. We have a room courtesy of the campaign where we can prepare ourselves as well as have our dinner. The Kennedy campaign lets us order room service. Our food was delivered by a young mexican boy named Juan. Juan and I engaged in a spanish dialogue about many things and mostly about his work at the hotel. My Spanish comes from having lived in East Los Angeles where almost all my good friends were Mexican. I also studied Spanish at Fairfax High.

Juan is excited and looks clean cut in his white waiter jacket. Juan has someone with him but that person remains quiet. All the conversation is between Juan and Myself. He probably needed help with the three dinner trays he is bringing us. I am checking everyone out. I TRUST NOBODY.

Juan gives us our dinner and hands me a pink hotel linen napkin which I promptly put down besides me and do not see again until June 5th. We are getting ready for an exciting evening and all of our prayers are for a victory for Bobby. It has always been hard to call him Bobby as I continue to call him Sen. Kennedy out of complete respect and love for this man. Now he is Bobby to everyone.

I am totally wired, as I have been for the entire time we performed, and I have been told to be careful not to create "too much" enthusiasm. I remember what it felt like at the first place we performed. I was totally energized and got the crowd almost out of control. I remember thinking this must have been how easy it was for Hitler who mesmerized people with his voice. I was spent after I kept the crowd going for well over an hour before the Senator arrived. I had the crowd yelling at the top of their lungs. Motivating a crowd was easy for me. I had done this time and time again. They yelled the birds out of the trees.

Sen. Kennedy finally arrived and the crowd went wild. It was right on the spot that I was admonished for being overly enthusiastic. They still thanked me for the rousing welcome. I was exhausted. Generally I was the only one that spoke while we always sang as a group. Jim loved to sing "This man's in love with you" by Herb Alpert who also grew up a couple blocks away from me in the "Fairfax" area.

Sen. Kennedy had walked through the Fairfax area and won over all of the Jewish population. We were busy performing somewhere. Our singing clothes consisted of orange sweaters and bright white jeans. It was definitely a look. They were paid for by a donor who was a friend of my manager Karl Bornstein.

I am nervous. Very nervous as the clock moves towards eight p.m. when we are scheduled to go on stage at the Embassy Ballroom. We had a walk through earlier and had also performed at the Cocoanut Grove the previous day. We sang with Andy Williams who joined us in a rendition of "This Man is your man" and everyone cheered. John Glenn joined us on stage. America's Hero. Many of the greatest entertainers were already in the hotel. A buzz was in the air and I was very very alert. I could not relax.

June 4, 1968 was countdown for me as I began to walk through the hotel looking for anyone or anything that seemed out of place. I saw the Colonial Room, walked through the ballroom staring into the eyes of any and all that seemed out of place. I was looking for a sign that would give away anyone there to harm our candidate.

After a long walk-around through the Colonial room where the press was hanging out, through the lobby, the Venetian room, and the main ballroom I began to slowly look inside the kitchen, pantry, and through the swinging doors that led to the stage. Something felt wrong and it was the Ace security guards. They were awful. They were like standing dummies. Checking out the girls.

In order to get into the kitchen, pantry, and this back part of the ballroom one had to have a security button. The guard was busy looking at the girls and was not doing his job. I began confronting him nicely at first and then aggressively. He looked amused since he stood at least six feet - two to my nine foot nine inches in height. He did not back off nor did I as this built up to a boiling point. I felt the area behind the stage as the most vulnerable and continued harassing him the entire night into June 5.

"The Sounds of Time" performed continuously from the start of the evening and the place was packed. As the lead for the group I spoke to the crowd and had them chanting "We Want Kennedy" "We Want Bobby" and they just chimed in. Louder and louder.

I was on stage when I decided to jump into the crowd and off the platform we were performing on. The first time I jumped off Rosemary Clooney, and the kids she brought, with her, began dancing with me. She was so great and the kids loved it. We danced a lot and even when I went back on stage she continued to dance with a beautiful smile on her face. I was not sure who the kids were.

Soon others began dancing around and an extremely old woman brought down the crowd as she danced the night away. The cameras were rolling. We had all the networks. We had media from Canada and just a lot of excitement.

I must have jumped off the stage 20 times, microphone in hand, or more as I began to focus on faces that seemed "blank" who did not seem to be part of the action. When we took a slight break I went back to work on the Ace Security Guard who can be seen talking to Thane Eugene Cesar in photos that have since been published widely. The guard finally said in so many words that if I continued to taunt him he would beat me up. I did not back down. I felt that I had finally got some energy out of him. He was like a sleeping dog all night.

<u>As the night wore on there was something inside me saying "figure out" where the attack is going to come from.</u> The crowd inside the ballroom was now packed and the fire marshals even warned those in charge that the situation had to change it was that crowded. All the while reports began to come in about the preliminary results of the vote in South Dokota, and California. People kept cheering. Bobby was winning.

As this vote tally kept coming in my concern grew larger and larger. My forays into the crowd continued and I ran from one spot to another in the hotel looking for any signs that things were not right. Oh yes the security guard just kept letting people in. <u>I began to push people out the doors.</u>

We kept singing right up to midnight and into June 5th my birthday. I turned 23 that night. I started to feel old as my inner voice grew louder and louder. Where are we vulnerable? I kept at it.

My singers, Gayleen and Jim, were on stage and some strangers just started jumping on stage. I decided finally that an attack was going to come from the rear of the stage so I got off the stage and stood by the curtain off the stage, and in front of the doors that led to the pantry.

As I stood there Bobby Kennedy, all smiles, was shaking hands as he made his way on stage. He stopped briefly, shook my hand, and said he appreciated what we had done for him.

He was aware of our group and it felt nice. As he moved towards the stage I shouted out: "MR PRESIDENT I WILL MEET YOU IN THE WHITE HOUSE!" He then stopped, turned back towards me and gave me a great big smile. As he made his way up the stage I was at the curtain looking up at him speak and then looked back at the doors behind me.

I then stood at the doors leading to he pantry. I was prepared to die. I would take the bullets I knew were coming. I had prepared myself for this ever since my father died of a brain tumor, at age 39, in Paris. I tried to become strong after he died and found a way to take pain and not flinch. I would be his shield. <u>Then someone stepped in.</u>

<u>To this day I do not know who this person was but he came up to me and said I would have to leave the spot I was standing on.</u> He then said I needed to take my group and go downstairs to a ballroom below where an overflow crowd of over 300 people had been waiting. He told

me Robert Kennedy would join me as soon as he finished speaking at the main ballroom. I resisted and he kept coming at me to move. I insisted in waiting for Sen. Kennedy but he kept promising I would see him soon. I looked at the stairs and then back.

I REMEMBER IT LIKE A VIDEO FILM

I looked at this stranger with the button on his lapel. I did not remember ever seeing him but that button looked official. I pulled the curtain back and motioned Jim and Gayleen to come with me down the stairs. The stairs led to the ballroom below and we descended quickly. It could not have taken more than 20 seconds. When I stepped on the stage I saw people in agony in front of me. Some were crying and some were fainting in front of us. 20 seconds. I turned to Jim and Gayleen and said it's over. I told them that he was dead. I had seen this, but like Cassandra, nobody believed.

I began to run back up the stairs we had just descended trying to get back up to the doors and the pantry. It was blocked. The Los Angeles Police Department was taking over. I could not figure out how they had come into this exact spot on the stairs. There were no police ever in sight during the entire night. They stopped me from going back up. How did they get here so fast?

I saw a door leading out and just slammed against it and began to run down the stairway on the side of the building. I saw a motorcycle cop hit the ground as he had made a sweeping move to turn. His gun was drawn. I was in the parking lot and began to run back through the entire car lot and raced towards the ballroom. People were crying and the place was a wreck with sobbing and angry people. Damn. I was very distraught.

I finally reached the kitchen and nearly assaulted the Ace Security Guard, Jack, and laid down a barage of anger towards him. I kept saying "I told you, I told you. You were not doing your job" Look what you did! I was besides myself. He looked down at me.

Then this Ace Security Guard said: "Don't worry, He is going to be OK, He has been shot in the leg and it was not life threatening." I was in total disbelief. I kept asking him if he was sure and he insisted that it was just a grazing shot to his leg. I turned with a sigh of relief and began going back to our room. There was nothing I could do. The place felt horrendous and I even went up to people repeating what I had heard. He had fooled me. I still see his face and hear those lying words. He was wrong all night long. Then he lied to me.

I went back to the room. There was still some dinner I had not even eaten half of my sandwich. I now pulled the linen napkin and opened it. I was startled. The young man had given us napkins but only mine was different. Inscribed with thread were the dates: 1963 and 1968 on opposite sides of the napkin. I had met President Kennedy in 1962 and everyone knew that 1963 was the year the president had been shot and killed. Now I was staring at an Ambassador Linen napkin with both dates on it. I felt sick.

NOW I WAS STARTLED

I felt like someone hit me in the stomach. 1963 was the year President Kennedy was assassinated in Dallas and now I was in 1968. This was odd and in very poor taste. I had the Television on in the room when all of a sudden my friend Gabor Kadar was being interviewed and he kept crying. He would speak a little and then begin crying a lot. He described where Robert Kennedy had been hit. Gabor had come to see us perform and could not get in. He, and another young man, both had the same idea. To reach into the dirty linen and put on a waiter's uniform so they could get in. The person he was now standing next to was Sirhan Sirhan. In every documentary he can be heard screaming "get the gun get the gun" and then pointing to his head as if saying he was shot in the head. Gabor had ended up

being where I wanted to be and he struggled
with Sirhan after he opened fire from quite a
distance. Eventually Roosevelt Grier and Rafer
Johnson pulled the gun from his hand. The
coroner thought the shot was an inch away
from RFK's head. Noguchi was assaulted by
those in power in Los Angeles. Powder burns!

I began to cry slowly and then like a river of
tears. It had happened exactly as I feared
it would. I was distraught and then angry. I
looked at the napkin and went downstairs.
I had to find out who would have done
something so crude. I walked over to the
bartender in the lobby next to the doors
leading to the Embassy Ballroom. I showed the
napkin to the bartender and asked him what
to make of it. Without hesitation he waved to a
man in a dark suit. The man identified himself
as the FBI and started to look at the napkin.
He also wanted to know where I got it and
I told him. I started to reach out to retrieve
the napkin but he put it in his pocket. I never

heard any more from the so-called FBI agent. The next day I went to the hotel management and asked them about the napkins and what happens to the old ones? They said they destroyed the old napkins at the end of each year and would never have two dates in either case. How was this possible. Had I been given a warning? 1963! Impossible was the reply.

I felt awful that I had that napkin taken away from me. At that moment I felt completely uneasy with any authority that talked to me afterwards. What happens next is truly unbelievable.

To this day I have never heard of anyone talking about that napkin with the year of the JFK assassination. He made sure nobody saw it again.

THE LOS ANGELES TIMES JUNE 5, 1968

The last words my father spoke to me was about how **bitter-sweet** life could be. He said I needed to appreciate both. He taught me a good lesson.

I went to visit my mother June 6, who lived in the "Fairfax" area and she showed me the front page of the Los Angeles Times. Our group was on the front page. She had noticed my being on stage at the Ambassador Hotel and just took a scissor and cut the front page in half. She handed it to me and I brought it home. The photo showed our group on stage about five minutes before Sen. Kennedy arrived to give his victory speech. My birthday, June 5, 1968, and the headline read:

SEN. KENNEDY SHOT AT VICTORY FETE

I had been interviewed by Jack Smith of the Los Angeles Times and he had asked me why I liked Kennedy. I told him that he reminded me of the great qualities Abraham Lincoln had. He seemed a little put off by my answer and it never appeared anywhere in the paper. I guess it was too innocent.

So I am at the Los Angeles Times and I ask the clerk if she could please get me the June 5, 1968 edition. I wanted a copy of the photo of our group on stage. She looked at me funny. She pulled the June 5 edition and told me that what I was asking for did not exist. I told her they probably ran two papers that day and she insisted there was only one. Now I did not even trust the L.A. Times. I began to distrust everyone. What was in that edition that they were afraid of? Where was my linen napkin and then the next series of photos shows Juan Romero giving Bobby Kennedy Rosary beeds while a <u>tie</u> belonging to an Ace Security guard lies next to him on that blood drenched floor. How did the LAPD get there so fast.

Years later a retired LAPD officer who had just joined the police force in 1968, told me that things were very strange. He also told me that a detective, named Manuel Pena, who was working the Kennedy case, was most likely been a member of the C.I.A. He and another police officer were the ones who made the lives of the witnesses quite difficult. Hernandez was the other detective.

THE SOUNDS OF TIME FOUR MINUTES TO MIDNIGHT

June 5, 1968

Left to right: ABC cameraman, Leon, Kris Desautelles, Jim on Guitar at the Embassy Ballroom 5 minutes before Kennedy's victory speech. The lady at the Los Angeles Times said the edition was never printed. Really? Here it is.

My mother cut it out and saved it for me. Now I trusted nobody. There were at least two editions that ran on June 5th. Who took the original?

Here is a copy of that front page

I WENT TO THE YOUNG ARCHIVAL BUILDING ON AUGUST 17, 2014 AND FOUND THAT THE PHOTOS THEY HAD WERE ALMOST IMPOSSIBLE TO LOOK THROUGH.

THEY WERE NOT ORGANIZED.

I THOUGHT PERHAPS THE POLICE TOOK THAT ORIGINAL TO LOOK AT THE THOUSANDS OF PEOPLE WHO WERE AT THE BALLROOM THAT NIGHT.

UNLIKE SCOTT ENYART THAT PHOTO DID NOT BELONG TO ME. SCOTT ALSO WENT TO FAIRFAX HIGH SCHOOL.

SCOTT WAS IN THE ROOM AND THE POLICE TOOK HIS NEGATIVES AND THEN THEY WERE STOLEN FROM A CAR.

THIS PHOTO PRESERVES A MOMENT IN OUR HISTORY.

THE SOUNDS OF TIME

MAGICAL

"COMMUNICATION" WAS THE NAME OF OUR NEW STORE

ELLIOT AND JACK GILBERT AND I WERE PARTNERS IN THAT ENTERPRISE.

THE SOUNDS OF TIME AND SOME MAGIC

Do you believe in magic? I never really thought about it but in 1968 there was some magic working. It was like no other year I had experienced. I was singing solo and sounded a lot like Bob Dylan who I would listen to every day at lunch at Cal State Los Angeles where I was studying. I found his lyrics penetrated deep within my soul. Dylan just was my hero.

Karl Bornstein, a Fairfax High friend, was my manager and he enjoyed my impromptu singing in places like the Troubador as well as that great place the Ash Grove on Melrose which is now the Comedy Store. A couple friends who came over on the boat, Jack and Elliot Gilbert, and I opened what was then called a Head Shop. We would get the spill-over crowd from the Ash Grove and many top musicians would come in. People like Taj Mahal and The Nitty Gritty Dirt Band would stop in, look around, and then pull out their instruments and play. We had a grand opening which included over

500 people who spilled out into the street. The sixties were happening everywhere.

Karl called me up and asked if I would like to see Robert F. Kennedy at an SRO event at the Sports Arena which was downtown Los Angeles. He said everyone was going to be there including Sony and Cher, The Byrds, Maharishi, Shirley MacLaine and so many other top entertainers. When I got there the crowd was estimated at 15,000 screaming fans of Bobby Kennedy.

Karl tapped me on the shoulder and said: "Too bad you don't have a singing group. If you did you could go on tour with Robert Kennedy and join his quest for the White House." I asked him how many days I had and he said three days. I would have two days to practice and then audition with Mrs. Ethel Kennedy and Jerry Bruno.

I stood up and walked towards the stage and stopped about four yards away from where Senator Kennedy was looking out at the crowd. I stood perfectly still and raised my right hand in a peace sign and stood there waiting. Bobby looked over the crowd and then saw me. I thought standing still was a good idea since everyone else was jumping up and down screaming. He stood for a moment and then held out his right hand in a peace sign and pointed right at me. I had connected which I felt I needed. I ran back to karl and told him I would be ready in two days. I had virtually nobody to call. I did not know any other musicians. This kind of magical experience seemed to happen a lot to me since my father died.

After the event I went home to my apartment in west los angeles and pulled out one of those huge Yellow Pages and placed it on the dining room table. I took a deep breath and opened the book in half. I then closed my eyes and put my finger on the page and looked at the name Gayleen Woodruff. I called and she answered the phone. She asked who I was and I told her Vaiz Meehr. She thought she knew me and that somehow I had reminded her of Meher Baba. In

Yiddish Vaiz Meehr means "Oh My God." I grew up speaking both Yiddish and French.

After a brief conversation I asked her if she was a singer and she replied that she was and I told her about the singing group for Robert Kennedy and she was floored. Yes. Yes she replied. I am in.

The previous week I had been to KTLA television studios on Sunset Boulevard. I was looking for work and the nice woman said there were no opening but then she told me about her son who was coming from Massachusetts and was both a guitar player and singer. Her son was Jim Wolk. I had stuck the phone number in my pocket and pulled it out after I had called Gayleen. Jim and I hit it off immediately. Jim, Gayleen, and I rehearsed THIS MANY IS YOUR MAN which was a take on Woody Guthries song "This Land Is Your Land."

We rehearsed for one day and we sounded like a group that had been together for years.

Our energy was also great. We entered a room where Mrs. Kennedy and Jerry Bruno were seated. Jerry Bruno had been President Kennedy's advance man and now he was working with Robert Kennedy. We began singing and Mrs. Kennedy and Jerry looked at each other and half way through our song they stopped us and welcomed us to the campaign. We were now the official advance team performers in Southern California. We became the group called <u>THE SOUNDS OF TIME</u>. We hit the ground running and started out with one of our smaller crowds of 20,000. We were launched. We entertained over a hundred thousand through the streets of Los Angeles on a flat bed truck.

Photos by our friends.

Here we are at the Embassy Ballroom. I have literally jumped four feet off the ground. Jim is on Guitar on the right and Gayleen near the gloved person. Theodore Charach, who wrote the second gun theory and documentary can be seen in the crowd behind me and Gayleen. He is in many photos behind me.and documentary can be seen in the crowd behind me and Gayleen.

We were expected to not only sing but to create lots of energy with the audience. Once when we started I got the crowd too excited and was asked to bring it down a notch. The crowds were so very excited to see Bobby Kennedy. One had to be there to understand how rarified the air was. It was magic.

FORMER CONGRESSMAN JOE KENNEDY HELPS THE POOR.

Visiting the JFK Library I met Joe Kennedy, Lt. Governor Kathleen Kennedy Townsend and many other people who loved RFK. I told Joe that so many people tried to give me photos they took with a polaroid but I had nowhere to put them and I always thought there would be more time to take one with Bobby Kennedy but that proved elusive. He then put his arm around me and someone snapped this picture and made me happy.

I AM STILL LOOKING FOR THE RFK PHOTOS. If you are reading this book and have a photo of Myself with Robert Kennedy please get in touch. Look for a young man with a goatee. I know there are countless photos out there in America.

An image of Robert Kennedy. I am the only person that knows where it came from. It has never been published or seen before.

My father, Myself, and Mother standing next to

a memorial to the six million dead in Germany

Mendel, my father, was in the Polish Cavalry

The same cavalry which centuries before saved the

Roman Church in Vienna from the Ottoman Empire.

THE LAST PHOTO TOGETHER IN PARIS
MENDEL DIED DURING A BRAIN TUMOR
OPERATION. HE WAS 39 YEARS OLD.

THE HOSPITAL WAS SAL PATRIERE
WHERE I FOUND OUT MY WIFE'S
COUSIN WAS A DOCTOR. AMAZING.

A SEWING MACHINE LIKE THIS WAS HOW MY PARENTS MADE A LIVING

WHEN MY FATHER DIED I WENT UNDER HIS SEWING MACHINE FOR DAYS.

I CRIED AND WOULD NOT COME OUT TO EAT.
NOTHING COULD COMFORT ME.

NEXT YEAR IN JERUSALEM WAS WHAT I HEARD GROWING UP

NEVER FORGET ISRAEL.

"LET MY RIGHT ARM BE CUT OFF IF EVER DID."

Tough Neighborhood.

Germany-1947

Mendel/Leon Fajnstadt

MENDEL AND I IN GERMANY IN 1947. ROSE
SAID WE HAD NOTHING TO FEAR SINCE THE
AMEICAN SOLDIERS WERE IN CHARGE. AMERICA
BECAME OUR HOME AND NURTURED US.

MENDEL IS WEARING HIS MILITARY OUIFIT

THE AMBASSADOR HOTEL

AND

THE GOOD SAMARITAN HOSPITAL

JUNE 5-6 1968

HERE ARE PHOTOS TAKEN BY

DR. JAYSON SHER WHO
GRADUATED WITH MY CLASS AT
FAIRFAX HIGH SCHOOL IN 1964.

HE AND HIS FATHER WERE
PHOTOGRAPHERS AND
OFTEN WORKED AT THE
AMBASSADOR HOTEL

HE KNEW THE HOTEL INSIDE OUT.

HE WAS KIND ENOUGH TO ALLOW
ME TO USE THEM IN THIS BOOK.

THESE PHOTOS WERE KEPT IN AN
AIRTIGHT PLASTIC CASE FOR 46
YEARS. DR. SHER DESIGNED THE
CASE TO PRESERVE THE ITEMS HE
PHOTOGRAPHED AND COLLECTED.

THE AMBULANCE

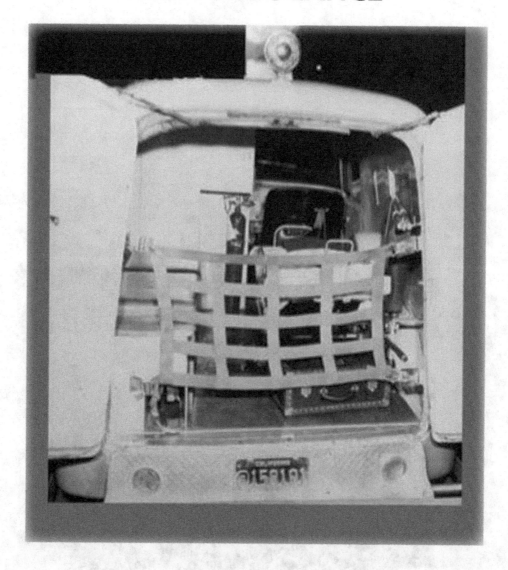

This ambulance took Robert Kennedy to the hospital.

GOOD SAMARITAN SIGN

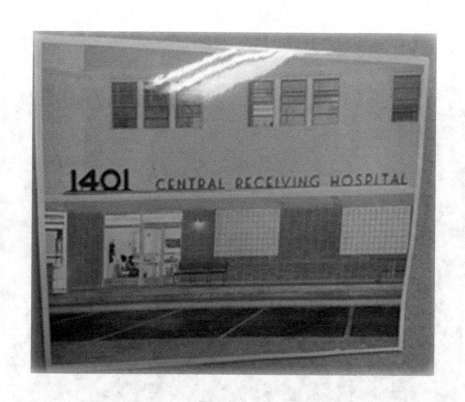

EMERGENCY ROOM

GOOD SAMARITAN

GOOD SAMARITAN FRONT ENTRANCE

PHOTO AFTER THE CROWD IS GONE

THE TRAGEDY. ONE CAN FEEL IT.

BULLET HOLES DRAWING BY DR. SHER

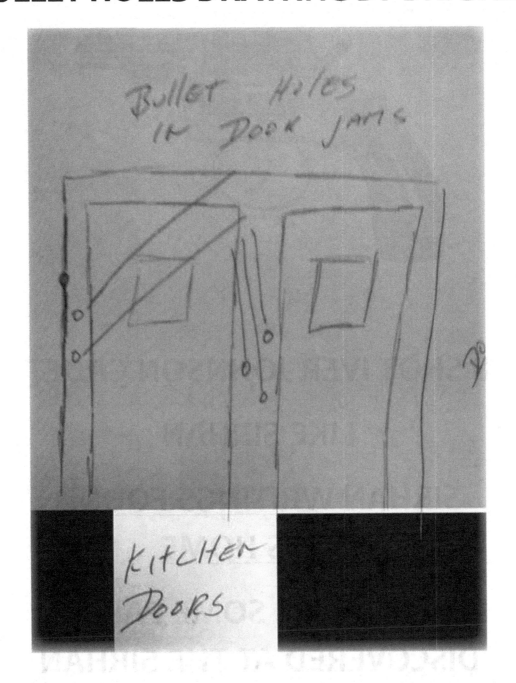

Bullet Holes
in Door Jams

Kitchen
Doors

DRAWINGS AFTER SHOOTINGS

THE BULLET HOLES DID NOT ADD UP

22

8 SHOT IVER JOHNSON CADET

LIKE SIRHAN

<u>SIRHAN WRITINGS FOUND</u>
<u>IN HIS HOME</u>

THERE WERE SOME PAPERS
DISCOVERED AT THE SIRHAN
RESIDENCE IN PASSADEN.

REPETITIVE WRITING READ: MUST
KILL KENNEDY BEFORE JUNE 5, 1968

IF I FELT BAD BEFORE THEN
THIS PUT IT OVER THE TOP.

I UNDERSTOOD THE
CASSANDRA CURSE.

I HAD BEEN RIGHT ABOUT THE DATE
ALTHOUGH I FEARED THERE
WERE NO SAFE EXITS OUT OF
THAT HOTEL IF HE WON. HIS
INTEGRITY WAS TOO MUCH FOR
THOSE WHO WANTED WAR.

THE SOUNDS OF TIME

TRYING TO SAVE BOBBY

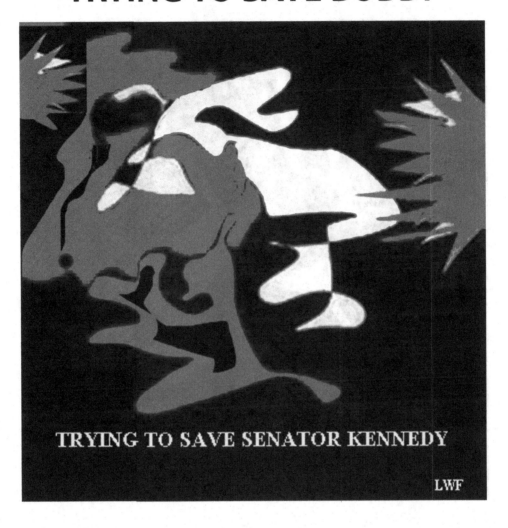

141

TRYING TO SAVE BOBBY 2

HOURS OF TAPES MADE

BY DR. SHER

4 HOURS OF TAPE MADE ON

JUNE 5, 1968

AMBASSADOR PAPER NAKINS

KENNEDY ITINERARY

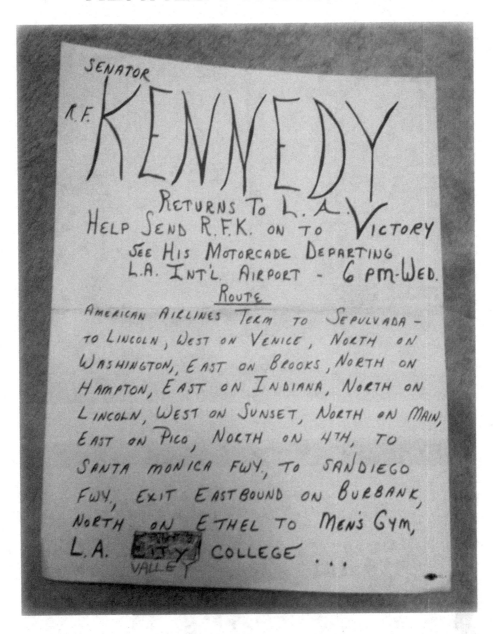

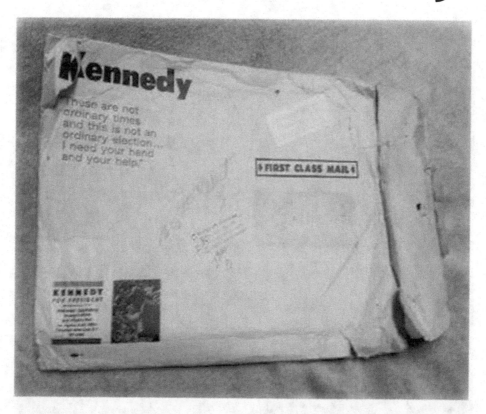

Rosemary Clooney

I UNDERSTAND THE ROSEMARY CLOONEY SUFFERED DEEPLY

SHE WAS AN AMAZING HUMAN BEING AND TALENT. SHE HAD A BUNCH OF KIDS WITH HER AND WE ALL DANCED.

I danced with Rosemary Clooney for a long time.

Our group on the dance floor

We kept the place jumping.

My guitar gave me a voice

THIS MAN IS YOUR MAN, THIS MAN IS MY MAN, FROM CALIFORNIA TO THE NEW YORK ISLANDS, FROM THE REDWOOD FORRESTS TO THE GULF STREAM WATERS..THIS MAN IS GOOD FOR YOU AND ME.

SONG FOR BOBBY THAT WE SANG. A GIFT TO US ALL FROM HIS GREAT WIFE, MRS. ETHEL KENNEDY. HE IS ALWAYS IN OUR HEARTS AND WE ARE THE RIPPLES THAT WILL FINISH THE WORK.

(A GIFT FROM WOODY GUTHRIE.

I LOVED ENTERTAINING PEOPLE

BEFORE THE GUITAR I WAS VERY VERY SHY.

SINGING FOR KENNEDY WAS A GREAT PRIVELEGE.

I BROKE OUT OF BEING SHY WHEN I SANG.

On the Floor / Embassy Ballroom

I AM NOT A DETECTIVE BUT HERE ARE SOME ITEMS OF INTEREST. LOTS OF THEORIES DID NOT CHANGE ANYTHING. MAYBE SOMETHING THAT I HAVE USED IN MAKING THIS BOOK MAY HELP SOMEONE FIND OUT WHO "THEY" WERE.

Somehow my mother was the only person in Los Angeles that saw this newspaper and cut it out because I was on the cover.

The Times said it never happened.

The Sounds of Time: Cover Photo

YOU GUESSED IT.

PERMISSION BEFORE PUBLISHING

Estimated Time taken: 12:04 AM

ON THE STAGE WERE:

MYSELF, GAYLEEN WOODRUFF, JIM WOLK AND A HOST OF PEOPLE WHO ENDED UP JUMPING ON THE STAGE.

I ALWAYS DRIVE BY THE HOTEL AND

SAY A PRAYER FOR BOBBY.

I FEEL LIKE I AM STILL
IN THAT HOTEL.

RICHARD MILHOUSE NIXON

AT THE BEGINNING OF HIS CAREER

WERE GAMBLERS AND CRIMINALS

DREW PEARSON PUT THE SQUEEZE ON PEOPLE IN POLITICS TO BE HONEST.

ONLY BIG PEOPLE

"NIXONS THE ONE" CAMPAIGN THEME

Mickey Cohen, Gangster

KENNED FOUGHT CRIME HIS ENTIRE CAREER NIXON WAS USING GANGSTERS AND MURRAY CHOTINER TO RAISE THOUSANDS EARLY IN HIS CAREER. NIXON WAS COZY WITH GANGSTERS.

MICKEY COHEN WAS BEATEN IN PRISON WITH A STEEL PIPE ON THE HEAD. I WONDER WHY?

CHECK OUT THE INFO AVAILABLE.

MICKEY COHEN TOOK OVER WHEN BUGSY SIEGAL WAS KILLED IN BEVERLY HILLS. BUGSYS SIEGEL STARTED THE LAS VEGAS PHENOMENON. MICKEY COHEN TOOK OVER WHEN BUGSY WAS SHOT IN BEVERLY HILLS.

MORE NIXON

NIXON PARDONED JIMMY HOFFA. IT WAS SAID HE DID SO FOR $500,000.

WELL CAN YOU IMAGINE THAT? JIMMY HOFFA DISSAPPEARED SHORTLY AFTER LEAVING PRISON TO NEVER BE HEARD FROM OR SEEN EVER AGAIN.

THESE CROOKS CLEANED UP. WHEN MICKEY COHEN WAS DOUBLE CROSSED HE SPOKE TRUTH TO POWER. HE SAID NOBODY WILL EVER FIND JIMMY HOFFA'S BODY. HIS BEATING WAS DEVASTATING AND HE WAS NEVER THE SAME AGAIN. THAT WILL TEACH PEOPLE

TO NEVER RAISE MONEY FOR CROOKS.

Chotiner Threats

Nixon All the time

CHOTINER WAS NIXON'S FRONT MAN AND THERE WASN'T A CROOK HE DID NOT REPRESENT. HE WAS NIXON'S CHIEF OF STAFF.

MICKEY COHEN ON HOFFA.

"HE FELL INTO A TRAP."

THEN SOMETHING REALLY ODD HAPPENED.A YOUNG MEXICAN BOY WAS DETAINED IN JUAREZ, MEXICO SHORTLY AFTER JUNE 5, 1968

CRISPIN CURIEL GONZALEZ DETAINED IN JUAREZ MEXICO WHEN A LETTER FELL FROM HIS POCKET IMPLICATING HIM IN THE ROBERT F. KENNEDY ASSASSINATION

THEN THE COVER UP BEGAN

YOUNG MEXICAN BOY AND MEXICO

HAS ANYONE EVER HEARD OF THIS CASE.

JULY 6, 1968 / JUAREZ MEXICO

JULY 6, 1968

HEADLINE: JUAREZ POLICE HOLDING YOUTH IN RFK CASE

On June 17, 1968 a young mexican boy dropped a letter in Juarez Mexico. 17 year old Cristin Curiel Chacon has been implicated in the assassination of Robert Kennedy. It is said he had knowledge of the assassination.

The Mexican Federal District Attorney's office said they may have a prosecutable case.

THEN THE SLAMMER

HEADLINE: MEXICAN YOUTH WITH RFK ASSASSINATION LETTER HANGS HIMSELF.

CRISTIN CURIEL CHACON HAD BEEN SENT TO A PSYCHIATRIST BUT APPARENTLY WAS ABLE TO FASHION A ROPE MADE OUT OF STRIPS OF CLOTH TORN FROM A MATTRESS IN THE CELL.

HOW CONVENIENT.

HOW DOES SOMEONE DROP A LETTER IMPLICATING HIMSELF IN KILLING R.F.K.?

THE LAPD INVESTIGATION WAS WORSE.

BY THE WAY

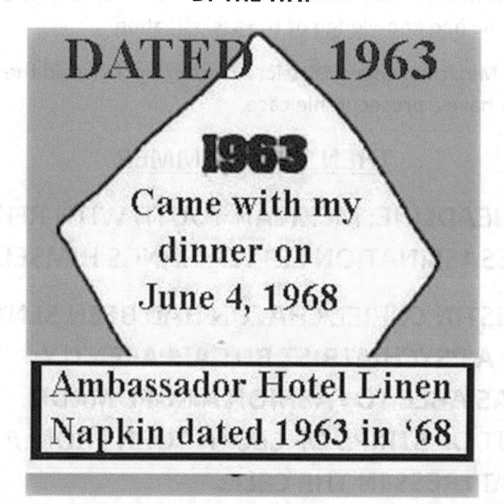

OUR GROUP, THE SOUNDS OF TIME, WERE SERVED
DINNER BEFORE DEPARTING TO ENTERTAIN THE CROWD
AT THE EMBASSY BALLROOM. WE WERE EXCITED.

THE PERSON WHO SERVED OUR DINNER MAY HAVE BEEN

ONE OF THE YOUNG MEN WHO STAFFED THE KITCHEN.

I SPOKE WITH ONE BRIGHT YOUNG PERSON
WHO WAS SO EXCITED TO BE SERVING THE
KENNEDY STAFFERS AND ADVANCE PEOPLE.

READ ON.

WHATS WRONG WITH THIS HOTEL NAPKIN?

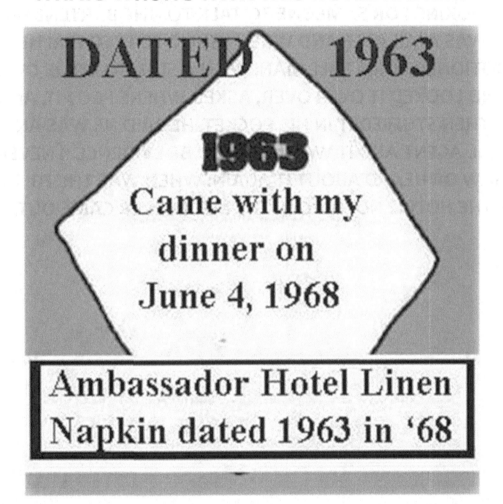

DATED 1963

1963
Came with my
dinner on
June 4, 1968

Ambassador Hotel Linen
Napkin dated 1963 in '68

I WAS NOT AWARE IMMEDIATELY OF WHAT WAS INSIDE THE WRAPPED HOTEL LINEN NAPKIN BUT AFTER THE ASSASSINATION I WENT BACK TO OUR ROOM, TURNED ON THE T.V. AND BEGAIN TO EAT THE REMAINDER OF MY SANDWICH.

WHEN I OPENED THE NAPKIN I NOTICED THAT THE YEAR 1963 WAS SEWN INTO THE CORNER OF THE NAPKIN. 1963?

YOU GET THE PICTURE AT LEAST I DID. I MET PRESIDENT KENNEDY IN 1962 AND HE WAS ASSASSINATED IN 1963.

HAD THIS BEEN AN ATTEMPT TO SEND A MESSAGE TO US?

I GRABBED IT AND RAN DOWN TO THE EMBASSY BALLROOM LOOKING FOR SOMEONE TO TALK TO. THE BARTENDER WAS AVAILABLE AND WHEN I SHOWED IT TO HIM HE MOTIONED FOR A TALL MAN, WITH A SUIT, TO COME OVER AND LOOKED IT OVER OVER, ASKED WHERE I GOT IT, AND THEN STUFFED IT IN HIS POCKET. HE SAID HE WAS AN F.B.I. AGENT AND IT WAS GOING TO BE EVIDENCE. I NEVER SAW OR HEARD ABOUT IT AGAIN. WHEN WAS THE FBI IN THE HOTEL? NOTHING IN THE MEDIA EVER CAME OUT.

LOS ANGELES MEMORIAL SPORTS ARENA

15,000 PEOPLE WERE AT THIS EVENT

FRIDAY MAY 24TH 1968 – 8PM

CAROL CHANNING, SONNY AND CHER, JERRY LEWIS, ROOSEVELT GRIER, GENE BARRY, HENRY MANCINI, TEDDY NEELY, SHIRLEY McCLAINE, ANGIE DICKINSON, ALAN KING, ANDY WILLIAMS, MAHALIA JACKSON, THE BYRDS, GENE KELLY, THE MAHARISHI

THIS IS WHERE I MADE

A CONNECTION TO

ROBERT F. KENNEDY.

TED CHARACH: THE SECOND GUN THEORY

I DID NOT KNOW TED BUT HE WAS RIGHT BEHIND ME ON THE BALLROOM FLOOR. HE CAN BE SEEN IN ALMOST ALL OF THE PHOTOS.

HE MADE A DOCUMENTARY FILM WHICH PROVED THE THANE EUGENE CESAR LIED WHEN HE SAID HE SOLD HIS 22 PISTOL BEFORE JUNE 5, 1968

HE SOLD IT MANY MONTHS AFTER.

HE WAS A BIGGOT AND A LIAR WHO HATED BLACK PEOPLE AND WAS A GEORGE WALLACE SUPPORTER.

HE DID NOT LIKE THE KENNEDY FAMILY.

THE SCREENING OF THE ACE SECURITY COPS WAS ESPECIALLY DISGUISTING.

KAZAKHSTAN IS WHERE I WAS BORN. IT WAS THE LOCATION OF THE BLAST OFF INTO SPACE FOR YURI GARGARIN. HE WAS THE FIRST MAN IN SPACE.

YOU CAN IMAGINE WHAT A HERO HE BECAME.

KAZAKHSTAN ALSO FOR TESTING NUCLEAR WEAPONS

KAZAKHSTAN WAS THE PLACE, IN SIBERIA, WHERE PEOPLE BECAME SLAVES. I WAS BORN A SLAVE.

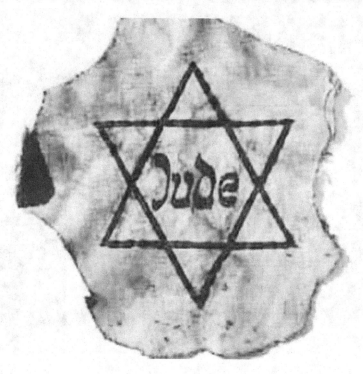

THERE WERE LOTS OF JUDE WHO DIED
IN THE GULAG FROM LACK OF FOOD TO
ILLNESS AND FROM THE BITTER COLD.

SEVENTY-FIVE PERCENT OF THE GULAG INMATES

DIED FROM LACK OF FOOD AND LACK OF MEDICINE

**OR THEY WERE JUST WORKED TO DEATH. MY
MOTHER AND FATHER WERE THE LUCKY ONES.
I WAS EVEN LUCKER TO BE BORN THE DAY THE
WAR IN EUROPE WAS OFFICIALLY OVER.**

ON ANOTHER FRONT
PEOPLE KEPT SEARCHING
FOR THE TRUTH

ABOUT THE R.F.K. ASSASSINATION

SEARCHING FOR TRUTH

FORMER CONGRESSMAN ALLARD LOWENSTEIN.

ALLARD LOWENSTEIN AND PAUL SCHRADE

AS WELL AS OTHERS ACROSS THE COUNTRY

AND THE WORLD.

Robert F. Kennedy Assassination

Lowenstein was one of the most vocal critics of the unwillingness of Los Angeles and Federal authorities to reopen the investigation into the June 6, 1968 assassination of Senator Robert F. Kennedy. Lowenstein's one-hour appearance on the PBS television show Firing Line in 1975, where he was interviewed by William F. Buckley Jr., was one of the first times the American public were shown that many elements of ballistic and forensic evidence were radically at odds with eyewitness testimony and the assumption that Sirhan Sirhan alone had shot Senator Kennedy.

YOU MAY NOTICE THAT NOTHING ABOUT THIS BOOK IS IN A STRAIGHT LINE.

THAT IS ON PURPOSE. OPEN TO ANY PAGE.

<u>GREG STONE</u>

For years, he had his mind on one thing: the assassination of Robert Kennedy. He spent almost every waking hour studying the case, and his apartment was a cross between an RFK shrine and archive. Then, last month, apparently despondent over his failure to reopen the case, Greg Stone killed himself.: The Obsession L.A. TIMES

GARY ABRAMS STAFF WRITER

I WISH I KNEW ABOUT GREG STONE.

SEARCH FOR THE USC LIBRARY WHERE THERE IS AN EXTENSIVE GREG STONE INFORMATION CATALOGUE. GREG WAS A WARRIOR.

A Lesson from my father to all children.
On June 5th in 1945, Under the sign of Gemini,
On the last day of the Second World War,
In a slave labor camp, I came into this world.
June 5th would come to represent the "Sweet and the Sour"
reality of life that my father taught me about before
he died of a brain tumor at age 39. June 5, 1968 was
that kind of day. Kennedy won and we lost him.

Leon / Sunset Strip / June 1967

ONE YEAR BEFORE WORKING IN THE KENNEDY CAMPAIGN

I GUESS I THOUGHT I WAS COOL. PRETTY SKINNY.

PRAYER OF ST. FRANCIS

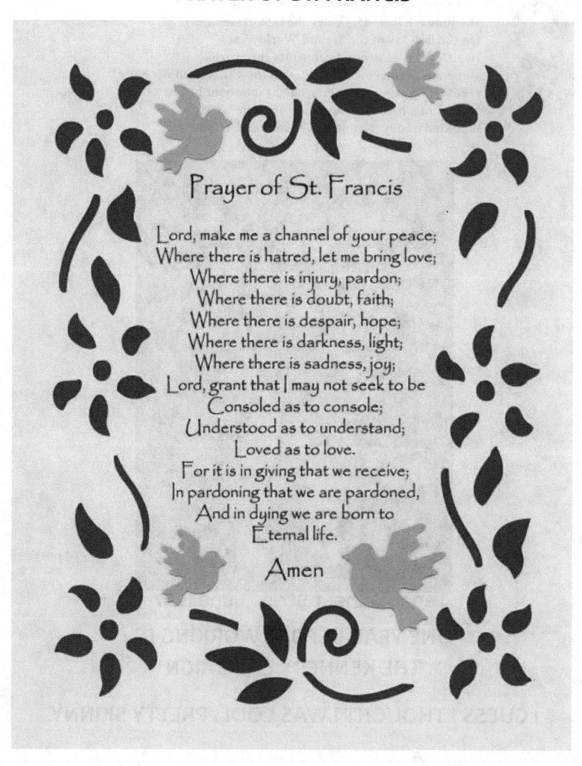

Prayer of St. Francis

Lord, make me a channel of your peace;
Where there is hatred, let me bring love;
Where there is injury, pardon;
Where there is doubt, faith;
Where there is despair, hope;
Where there is darkness, light;
Where there is sadness, joy;
Lord, grant that I may not seek to be
Consoled as to console;
Understood as to understand;
Loved as to love.
For it is in giving that we receive;
In pardoning that we are pardoned,
And in dying we are born to
Eternal life.

Amen

FRANCE

TITRE D'IDENTITÉ
ET
DE VOYAGE

Taxe : 580 francs

TITULAIRE :

Nom : FAJNSZTAJT

Prénoms : Rozia   né WALKER

Ce titre d'identité et de voyage comprend
18 pages non compris la couverture

VOYAGE: PASSPORTS

WE LEFT PARIS WITHOUT

MY FATHER WHO IS BURIED

IN BANOLET CEMETARY

HE WAS 39 YEARS OLD WHEN HE DIED.

REAR EXIT, THE AMBASSADOR, BACK STAIRS

EXIT FROM THE BOTH BALL ROOMS.
THIS IS WHERE MS. SERRANO WAS
SITTING WHEN THEY SAID <u>WE SHOT HIM</u>.
SHE SAID WHO? REPLY KENNEDY.

FOOTBALL WAS MY PASSION IN
HIGH SCHOOL AND IN COLLEGE.
I PLAYED LINEBACKER, CENTER, AND
DEFENSIVE END. I WAS AN ALL-LEAGUE PLAYER.

I LOVED WATCHING THE KENNEDY
FAMILY PLAYING FOOTBALL. I DID
PLAY CATCH WITH ROSIE GRIER.

HOW TO GO FORWARD

IMAGINE MEETING JOHN GLENN

THE FIRST MAN IN SPACE

AND HAVING LEFT KAZAKHSTAN

WHERE THE FIRST RUSSIAN
WAS LAUNCHED INTO SPACE.

I MET THE FIRST AMERICAN IN
SPACE. HE IS GREAT. MEETING SEN.
JOHN GLENN WAS A HIGH MARK
FOR ME. HE IS COURAGEOUS.

VISITING BOBBY'S GRAVE WAS HARD

I COULD NOT STOP CRYING

"RIPPLES OF HOPE"

RIPPLE OF HOPE

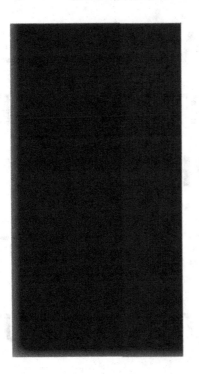 

I WAS INVITED TO THE WHITE HOUSE DURING

GEORGE H.W. BUSH'S TERM

THE STAFF, MYSELF, AND VALENTINO A FRIEND, MET IN

THE ROOSEVELT ROOM

I BEGAN TO CRY UNCONTROLLABLY

I REMEMBER SAYING TO BOBBY, THAT I WOULD SEE HIM IN THE WHITE HOUSE. I WAS OVERWHELMED.

I WAS THERE HE WAS NOT.

THE MEETING WAS ABOUT EDUCATION WHEN I FINALLY GOT MYSELF IN CONTROL.

HAYM SOLOMON / AMERICAN HERO

HAYM WAS ONE OF MY HEROES. HE HELPED GEORGE WASHINGTON AND HIS TROOPS WHEN THEY NEEDED FINANCIAL ASSISTANCE. HE SAVED THE AMERICAN REVOLUTION. HE WAS A POLISH IMMIGRANT OF JEWISH DESCENT. THIS STATUE IS IN PAN PACIFIC PARK IN LOS ANGELES. HE IS VERY SPECIAL

THE FREEDOM TRAIL CORPORATION

FOR EDUCATION

1990   LEON W. FAINSTADT

**THIS EFFORT GOT ME IN TOUCH
WITH THE WHITE HOUSE, THE PEROT
GROUP, <u>AND A YOUNG GOVERNOR</u>
<u>FROM ARKANSAS, BILL CLINTON.</u>**

THAT IS ANOTHER AMAZING STORY
ABOUT BEING ABLE TO SEE THE FUTURE
WITHOUT EFFORT. IT ALL JUST HAPPENED
AND I COULD NOT EXPLAIN IT.

IT STARTED OUT ABOUT EDUCATION

IT IS A GIFT. I WALKED UP TO A POSTER THAT HAD 50 U.S.GOVERNORS AT A WHITE HOUSE MEETING.

I LOOKED IT OVER, FOR LESS THAN A MINUTE, THEN TURNED TO MY CLIENT AND POINTED TO A MAN I HAD NEVER SEEN BEFORE AND SAID THESE EXACT WORDS.

LOOK AT THE NEXT PRESIDENT OF THE UNITED STATES.

WHAT HAPPENED NEXT IS A TRULY AMAZING.

I SENT A FAX TO GOVERNOR CLINTON IN ARKANSAS AND ASKED HIM WHAT HIS GOALS WERE FOR EDUCATION. I RECEIVED A GREAT LETTER BACK.

I LATER THAT YEAR WENT TO THE WHITE HOUSE AS WELL AS HAD A MEETING WITH THE DEPARTMENT OF EDUCATION. THAT BELT BUCKLE WAS THE FREEDOM TRAIL CORPORATE EFFORT ON BEHALF OF EDUCATION.

IT DID NOT STOP THERE. I THEN ASKED A FRIEND FROM JAPAN IF HE COULD INTRODUCE ME TO THE PEROT GROUP IN TEXAS. I DID SO BECAUSE I KNEW THAT ROSS PEROT WAS A STRONG ADVOCATE FOR GOOD EDUCATION. MY GOAL WAS A CROSS COUNTRY TRAIN RIDE FOR

EDUCATION. IT WAS A BIG PROJECT WHICH ALSO ATTRACTED PEOPLE FROM OTHER COUNTRIES LIKE SAUDI ARABIA FOR ONE. ONE OF THE SONS OF THE KING OF SAUDI ARABIA WAS VERY INTERESTED IN PAYING FOR AN ENTIRE TRAIN RIDE ACROSS AMERICA.

I SPENT A GOOD DEAL OF TIME TALKING ABOUT TOWN HALL MEETINGS WHERE POLITICIANS AND REGULAR FOLKS WOULD WORK ON IMPROVING EDUCATION.

I HEARD BACK FROM THE PEROT GROUP AND THEY POLITELY PASSED ON BEING INVOLVED.

I CALLED MY ATTORNEY AND TOLD HIM ROSS PEROT WAS GOING TO ANNOUNCE HIS CANDIDACY FOR THE WHITE HOUSE.

HE SAID IT WAS IMPOSSIBLE. THE NEXT DAY MR. PEROT ANNOUNCED HIS CANDIDACY. THAT MAN IN THE POSTER, I FOUND OUT WAS WILLIAM JEFFERSON CLINTON WON THE PRESIDENCY.

SOMEHOW I WAS CREATING RIPPLES OF HOPE AND I KNEW I MUST HAVE BEEN GUIDED BECAUSE WHO WOULD BELIEVE ME IF I TOLD THEM.

ROSS PEROT WON 19% OF THE VOTE WHICH KNOCKED OFF PRESIDENT BUSH.

THE GULF WAR NIXED THE CROSS COUNTRY TRAIN PROJECT BUT THERE IS ALWAYS NEXT TIME. I NEVER EVER GIVE UP ON SOMETHING GOOD.

IN THE MEAN TIME PRESIDENT CLINTON HAD QUITE A RIDE IN THE WHITE HOUSE. THE PEROT GROUP IS DOING WELL AND PRESIDENT BUSH JUST KEEPS JUMPING OUT OF AIRPLANES TO TEACH US TO STAY YOUNG FOREVER.

HOW CAN I EXPLAIN THE THINGS I HAVE DONE

I WANTED TO EXPLAIN HOW I WAS ABLE TO CRY OUT THAT BOBBY KENNEDY HAD JUST KILLED HIMSELF. IT IS NOT SOMETHING THAT I CONTROL.

I ONCE WENT TO SEE A DODGER GAME AND TOLD MY FRIEND WE WERE GOING TO SEE A NO-HITTER. MAYBE IT HELPED THAT **SANDY KOUFAX** WAS PITCHING BUT IT HAPPENED JUST LIKE THAT.

FINDING MY FATHER'S GRAVE IN PARIS, FRANCE WAS ANOTHER SUCH AMAZING EXPERIENCE SINCE I WAS GOING TO BE THERE ON MY 39TH BIRTHDAY. I DID NOT SPEAK FRENCH NOR DID I KNOW WHERE TO GO FIND HIS GRAVE. I PRAYED IN A HOTEL THAT BENJAMIN FRANKLIN HAD STAYED IN FOR STRENGTH. THEN I WALKED, TOOK BUSES AND TRAINS AND IN 6 HOURS FOUND HIS GRAVE SITE ON A SUNDAY WHEN MOST ALL STORES WERE CLOSED IN FRANCE. **I WAS 39 THE SAME AGE HE DIED. COINCIDENCE?** THE ENTIRE TRIP WAS PAID FOR BY AN AUSTRALIAN FILM COMPANY.

I PLAYED A HUNCH AND FOUND A STORE
WHERE THEY MADE HEADSTONES. I SPOKE
YIDDISH BECAUSE IT WAS A JEWISH CEMETARY.
THE WOMAN LOOKED IN THE BOOK AND SAID
THERE WAS NO CHANCE HE WAS BURIED
THERE.

I ASKED HER TO DRIVE ME TO THE CEMETARY
WHERE PEOPLE FROM CZESToCHOWA,
POLAND WERE BURIED. SHE DROVE AROUND
THEN STOPPED AND SAID: SEE IT IS NOT HERE.

HER SHOULDER UNDERLINED HIS NAME
BEHIND HER AS SHE SPOKE. ONE INCH TALLER
AND I WOULD NOT HAVE SUCCEEDED.

I BEGAN TO CRY TEARS OF JOY. IT HAD BEEN 34
YEARS SINCE I LAST SAW MY FATHER. HE WAS
BURIED IN A GRAVE WHERE 12 OTHERS WERE
BURIED.

I SAID A PRAYER IN SANSKRIT.

NAM MYOHO RENGE KYO.

NAM MYOHO RENGE KYO WHICH I HAD LEARNED SHORTLY AFTER BOBBY WAS ASSASSINATED. IT WAS A PRAYER FOR WORLD PEACE. I WAS CALM.

SOMETIMES DANGEROUS WORLD

I HAVE FACED MANY DANGERS IN MY LIFE TIME. ONCE A MAN POINTED A GUN AT ME AND THEN JUST STOOD THERE. I LOOKED AT HIM AND SAID WHY WOULD YOU DO THIS? YOU DON'T EVEN KNOW ME. I THEN TOLD HIM HE MUST BE VERY ILL. I TOLD HIM I WAS UNAFRAID OF HIM. HE THEN PUT THE GUN AWAY AND SAID HE WAS JUST JOKING. I ASKED HIM OUT TO BREAKFAST TO TALK TO HIM ABOUT GETTING HELP.

ONE DAY I TRAVELED TO MADISON WISCONSIN. I HAD NEVER SEEN IT AND KNEW IT HAD A GREAT UNIVERSITY. WHEN I ARRIVED THERE WAS A FULL FLEDGED RIOT GOING ON. THE RIOT WAS ABOUT THE VIETNAM WAR.

I HAD MY GUITAR, WHICH HAD A BLACK CASE, AND SOME WHITE TAPE. THAT CASE BECAME THE BACKGROUND FOR A CROSS. IT WAS A BIG CHRISTIAN CROSS AND I JUST BEGAN WALKING IN BETWEEN THE POLICE AND THE RIOTERS. EVERYONE JUST STOPPED! NOBODY KNEW WHAT TO DO WITH SOMEONE WHO WANTED PEACE. IT WAS NOT PLANNED. IT JUST FELT LIKE THE RIGHT THING TO DO. FRONT PAGE OF THE MILWAUKEE JOURNAL. LOOKED REVOLUTIONARY.

WHY ALL OF THESE STORIES?

I WAS A COURTROOM ARTIST IN ST. PAUL MINNESOTA AND WAS DRAWING THE LEADERS OF THE AMERICAN INDIAN MOVEMENT WHILE THEY WERE ON TRIAL. I WAS INVITED TO THE A.I.M. OFFICE WHERE I SAT WATCHING THE INDIANS PLAYING CARDS. SUDDENLY ONE OF THEM PULLED OUT A 45 CALIBER PISTOL AND POINTED RIGHT IN MY FACE. HE THEN SAID: "YOU ARE AN F.B.I. AGENT AREN'T YOU? I LAUGHED AND TURNED THE TABLES AND TOLD HIM HE WAS TRYING TO COVER HIMSELF AND THAT HE WAS THE AGENT. HE PUT THE GUN AWAY AS NOBODY SEEMED TO EVEN NOTICE. HE WAS WORKING WITH DENNIS BANKS. SEVERAL WEEKS LATER HE WAS IN THE NEWSPAPER AND ON THE NEWS. **I HAD BEEN RIGHT. HE WAS AN F.B.I. INFORMANT. I WAS NEVER AFRAID OF HIM WITH HIS 45 PISTOL. THAT BOTHERED HIM.**

MY EXPERIENCES COME FROM A DEEP AWARENESS THAT I AM PROTECTED AND I WILL COMPLETE MY OWN PERSONAL MISSION AS A HUMAN BEING WHO WANTS TO LIVE ON A PLANET WHERE PEACE GROWS LIKE FRUIT ON A TREE. **EACH OF US ARE MAGICAL.**

WE NEED EQULITY FOR ALL
BEINGS ON THIS PLANET

WOMEN WOMEN WOMEN MUST GAIN EQUALITY.

THINK ABOUT IT WE ARE
FUNCTIONING AT HALF SPEED.

WE ARE OUT OF BALANCE.

**WE ARE WASTING HALF OF THE PLANET
BY NOT ALLOWING WOMEN TO SIT AT
THE HEAD OF THE TABLE IN ALL NATIONS
FOR ALL PURPOSES AS EQUALS.**

MEN SEEM TO HAVE A PROPENSITY FOR
VIOLENCE AND WARFARE. JUST LOOK
AROUND THE PLANET AND YOU WILL SEE
THE WARS THAT HOLD OUR WORLD BACK.

Koyaanisqatsi: World Out of Balance.

A Navajo word about our world.

My experience with Hubert H. Humphrey

I loved going to college. Los Angles City College, Cal-State Los Angeles, UC Berkeley, University of Wisconsin Stevens Point, College of Saint Teresa in Winona Minnesota, University of Wisconsin and I studied woodcarving in Bali.

We all know Nixon beat Hubert Humphrey to become the crook he said he wasn't. In 1972 Sen. George McGovern ran for President against Nixon.

I was in Winona, Minn. and I already saw special news reports about Watergate before it happened.

One day during the campaign I was asked if I could pick up former Vice-President Hubert H. Humphrey. Of course I said I would. You should have seen his face when I pulled up in my mustang to spend the day with him. He laughed, got in the car, and we began campaigning – just the two of us. Hubert

Humphrey was brilliant and he knew the names of the farmers, their children, and was pleasant to be around. We had a great time together and his being there brought out some McGovern backers and created new ones.

I took photos of him that I ended up sending to Mrs, Eleanor Mondale and Vice-President Mondale when President Carter was in the White House. We communicated for several years about art and education.

Mrs. Mondale was very helpful and connected me with groups that worked with artists in America.

She loved the photo of Vice-President Humphrey getting out of that small airplane in Winona.

HUBERT H. HUMPHREY WAS BRILLIANT AND GREAT IN PERSON TO BE AROUND.

I returned to Los Angeles in 1975. THEN I HAD SEVERAL OF THOSE EXPERIENCES THAT I HAVE MENTIONED. <u>SEEING TOMORROW AGAIN.</u>

I WAS LIVING IN VENICE, CALIFORNIA AND FELT MY LIFE WAS NOT GOING WHERE I WANTED.

I WENT TO THE BEACH, AT NIGHT, WITH MY DOG, DURING A POWERFUL STORM AND SAT ON THE

ROCKS AND DID A BUDDHIST PRAYER. THE WAVES WERE VERY LARGE AND CRASHED AGAINST THE ROCKS. I CHANTED TO CHANGE MYSELF. AFTER ABOUT AN HOUR OF THIS PRAYER I CLOSED MY EYES AND SAW A MIRROW WITH MY FACE REFLECTED IN IT. A SEAL HAD COME CLOSE TO US AND APPEARED TO WATCH ME. A GOOD SIGN.

SUDDENLY I SAW MY FACE IN THE MIRROR BEGIN TO BE COVERED IN BLOOD FROM THE HAIRLINE DOWN. I JUST WATCHED AS IF I WAS WATCHING A MOVIE. UNAFRAID.

I THEN PRAYED THAT I WOULD TAKE ANYTHING IF IT MEANT I COULD BECOME MORE AWAKENED.

THE NEXT DAY I WENT TO WORK AT AARON BROTHERS ART MART, HELPED JANE FONDA, WHO I REALLY LIKED, WITH SOME ART, GAVE HER A BOOK ABOUT FILM, WHICH HAD HER FAMILY IN IT AND QUIT MY JOB.

I WAVED GOOD-BYE TO MY FORMER BOSS WHO WAS A FRIEND AND JUMPED IN MY CAR A FREE MAN. SEVERAL BLOCKS LATER WHILE DRIVING PARALLEL TO THE BEACH A TOW TRUCK RAN A STOP SIGN AND I RECOGNIZED THIS AS THE MOMENT I HAD PRAYED

ABOUT. I IMMEDIATELY PUT MY HANDS IN FRONT OF MY FACE AND WAS KNOCKED UNCONSIOUS.

I AWOKE TO THE SOUND OF VOICES TRYING TO PRY ME OUT OF MY CAR. IT HAD BEEN TOTALLY DESTROYED. THE POLICE AND FIREMEN WERE GETTING THE DOOR OPEN AND I HAD A HUGE HEADACHE. I WAS PLACED ON THE SIDEWALK AND THERE WAS THAT BLOOD STREAMING DOWN MY FACE.

THE ONLY THING THAT SAVED ME WAS THE FACT THAT I PUT MY HANDS IN FRONT OF MY FACE INSTINCTUALLY AND THAT PRAYER AND VISION AT THE BEACH HAD SAVED ME. AS I WAS ON THE SIDEWALK I PRAYED TO STAY AWAKE AS I KNEW IF I FELL ASLEEP I WOULD BE DEAD. THAT SANSKRIT PRAYER KEPT ME AWAKE.

I WAS TAKEN, IN AN AMBULANCE, TO THE HOSPITAL AND THE FUNNY THING WAS THE PERSON THAT HIT ME LOOKED VERY FAMILIAR.

THE MAN SITTING ACROSS FROM ME IN THE AMBULANCE LOOKED LIKE HE SAW A GHOST.

IT WAS NOT MORE THAN A FEW MINUTES BEFORE THAT HE WAS TALKING TO MY MANAGER A HALF BLOCK FROM WHERE I HAD JUMPED IN MY CAR. HE GOT A CALL AND WAS RACING TO THE ACCIDENT

WHEN HE RAN THAT STOP SIGN AND CRASHED INTO MY CAR.

I HAD INJURED MY KNEES AND MY FACE. MY WIRE RIM GLASSES HAD CUT MY FACE AND THE IMPACT HAD THROWN ME INTO THE WINDSHIELD LIKE A RAG DOLL.

THAT MOMENT I MENTIONED WAS COMING AGAIN.

I HAD SURGERY ON MY MINISCUS AND WAS OUT COLD. WHEN I WOKE UP MY WIFE WAS SITTING ACROSS FROM ME. AS I WAS AWAKENING I WAS TEARING AT MY BANDAGES AND HAD TO BE HELD FROM DOING SO.

WHEN I STARTED TO WAKE UP I SUDDENLY YELLED OUT THAT HUBERT HUMPHREY HAD JUST DIED. MY WIFE WAS ASTONISHED AND SHE TURNED ON THE TELEVISION SET. THE NEWS WAS ABOUT THE DEATH OF HUMBERT H. HUMPHREY. I CANNOT EXPLAIN IT.

THESE EXPERIENCES HAVE HAPPENED TO ME ALL OF MY LIFE. A FEW HAVE SAVED MY LIFE. "KNOWING IS A POWERFUL EXPERIENCE." SO MANY STORIES SO LITTLE TIME. GUESS THIS BOOK IS A GOOD IDEA.

TOO MANY TO MENTION BUT ONE STANDS OUT.

IN 1975 I HAD THIS OVERPOWERING FEELING ABOUT GOING TO WESTWOOD, WHERE UCLA IS LOCATED, AND THAT FEELING WOULD NOT SUBSIDE.

I HOPED ON A BUS, SINCE I DID NOT HAVE A CAR, AND MET WITH A FRIEND FROM ARGENTINA WHO CUT HAIR IN THE VILLAGE BUT HIS LANGUAGE SKILLS WERE LACKING.

I TOLD HIM I WOULD FIND SOME CLIENTS FOR HIM. I BEGAN TO MEET YOUNG WOMEN WHO I INTRODUCED TO MY FRIEND. ONE OF THOSE WOMEN ENDED UP HAVING LUNCH WITH US. JANET, THAT WOMAN, AND I ENDED UP GETTING MARRIED. IT HAS NOW BEEN 39 YEARS. <u>KNOWING IS ABOUT TRUSTING YOURSELF.</u>

I LOVED UCLA AND HAD PERFORMED ONE OF MY FAVORITE SONGS DURING THE SIXTIES ON CAMPUS. IT IS CALLED <u>FAITH</u> AND IS ABOUT ALLOWING PEOPLE TO HAVE THE FREEDOM TO BELIEVE IN THEIR FAITH.

I AM SURE I LEFT OUT A LOT OF INTERESTING THINGS ABOUT MY EXPERIENCES.

AT LEAST NOW INSTEAD OF TALKING ABOUT MY EXPERIENCE IN THE KENNEDY CAMPAIGN I CAN

SPARE OUR DAUGHTER AND MY WIFE BY HANDING
SOMEONE A BOOK. I NEVER TIRE OF TELLING THE
STORY BUT THEY WILL FINALLY BE ABLE TO SAY:
READ THE BOOK.

I DO HAVE ONE MORE THING TO SHARE. WHILE
CROSSING THE ATLANTIC OCEAN THERE WAS AN
ALERT ABOUT THE SHIP SINKING.

THE SHIP WAS THE USS GENERAL BLATCHFORD.

NO MATTER HOW HARD THEY TRIED I WOULD NOT
PUT ON A LIFE JACKET. I TOLD MY MOTHER THAT
WE WOULD NOT SINK BECAUSE I HAD IMPORTANT
THINGS TO DO. SHE JUST SMILED AND LOOK: WE
MADE IT.

THAT SHIP WAS THE USS GENERAL BLACHFORD
WHICH TOOK OUR REMAINING FAMILY
ACROSS THE ATLANTIC TO ELLIS ISLAND ON
THANKSGIVING DAY.

FROM THE TROOPS IN EUROPE THAT HELPED US TO THE
TROOP TRANSPORT SHIP THAT BROUGHT US TO AMERICA
MY MOTHER, BROTHER, AND I THANK AMERICA.

MY FATHER MENDEL FAJNSTADT IS STILL WITH ME AND I
BELIEVE HE HAS SAVED MY LIFE OVER AND OVER AGAIN.
WHEN HE WAS IN THE HOSPITAL FOR BRAIN SURGERY
HE SAID REMEMBER TO BE ABLE TO TAKE THE BITTER
AND THE SWEET. HE THEN HANDED ME A BAR OF BITTER
SWEET CHOCOLATE. HE SMILED AND SAID ENJOY LIFE.

I HAVE A LOCK OF HIS HAIR THAT WAS GIVEN TO ME BY
MY MOTHER, ROSE, WHO BECAME A MEMBER OF THE
SCREEN ACTORS GUILD. SHE WAS AN AMAZING WOMAN.
BERL FAJERBERG, WHO SHE MARRIED ALWAYS MADE
SURE WE WERE SAFE AND SECURE AS WE GREW UP.

SWANSTARZ WAS MY FIRST BOOK.

SWANSTARZ IS ABOUT SAVING THE HUMAN
RACE CLIMATE CHANGE IS A REALITY

AL GORE POINTED US IN THE RIGHT DIRECTION

HIS FATHER SAID "LET THE
GLORY OUT" AND HE DID.

THE QUEEN OF ENGLAND IS
TRYING TO WAKE EUROPE

PRINCE CHARLES IS WORKING ON THE RAINFOREST

"THE LUNGS OF OUR PLANET"

SWANSTARZ IS A CHILDRENS BOOK FOR ADULTS.

R.F.K.'68 IS MY SECOND BOOK.

SEEING IS ABOUT TRUSTING YOURSELF.

IN MY LIFE I HAVE STRIVEN TO BECOME A RIPPLE
OF HOPE AS ROBERT KENNEDY SPOKE ABOUT

NEW YORK HARBOR WAS NEVER PRETTIER. THE STATUE OF LIBERTY WAS THERE TO GREET US.

THEN CAME ELLIS ISLAND. WE WERE HOME.

WE LINED UP FOR THE POWDER AND THE USUAL
CHANGE OF THE SPELLING OF OUR NAME. POLISH
WAS A TOUGH CALL. SO WE DROPPED THE "J" AND
THE "Z" AND BECAME OFFICIALLY FAINSTADT.

I WAS 5 YEARS OLD AND TO THINK THAT IN
TWELVE YEARS I WOULD MEET THE PRESIDENT
OF THE UNITED STATES WAS AMAZING.

PRESIDENT KENNEDY AND HIS BROTHER SAVED THE
PLANET. ROBERT KENNEDY BECAME AN ENVOY PEACE
AND HELPED DELIVER THE AGREEMENT TO END THE
STALEMATE BETWEEN RUSSIA AND THE USA

<u>WE MAY WAIT GENERATIONS BEFORE
WE SEE THEIR LIKES AGAIN.</u>

ONE OF THE FAMILIES, THE GILBERTS, BECAME
OUR FRIENDS AND TO THIS DAY ELLIOT GILBERT
GILBERT AND I ARE FAMILY OR MESPUCHA.

Leon Wolf Fainstadt

Humanitarian, Artist, Author

Born: Dzhambul, Kazakhstan

June 5, 1945 Born A Slave to Slaves

Kazakhstan is the place the Soviets exploded
Nuclear Weapons. Societ citizens are still showing
the effects of radiation and are born disfigured.

RFK HAD NO CHANCE AFTER BEING SHOT.

On June 8, 1968 the attending surgeon, Dr. James L. Poppen, spoke of his experience in the ICU at Good Samaritan. He had been flown in by Mrs. Jacqueline Kennedy to attend to Robert Kennedy along with the other surgeons from the hospital.

What everyone present saw was the devastating result of a bullet that had penetrated the mastoid bone area and inflicted major damage to the pons and midbrain center of the brain.

DR. POPPEN PRAYED FOR HIM TO DIE. He knew, after a 10:AM operation that his wound was fatal.

"This is very hard to write but I feel it is important for others to know what happened after Bobby Kennedy was brought to the hospital."

By 6:30 PM, Wednesday, 18 hours after he was shot all legal requirements for death, his brain waves, could not be recorded. His vital organs began shutting down. Finally Robert F. Kennedy's life came to an end.

The bullet had penetrated the vital communication of the brain and thus the damage was catastrophic.

Robert F. Kennedy's body was flown to New York City at the request of Vice President Humbert H. Humphrey for a special memorial mass at St. Patricks Cathedral. He lay in repose from 10:00PM to 10:00AM on June 8, 1968.

"When I visited the graves of President Kennedy and Robert Kennedy there were enough tears to last a lifetime. I fell apart." Both had saved our nation from a Catastrophic Nuclear War. We owe them.

Imagine being born in the place where the space race began and then meeting Sen. John Glenn the first American astronaut to go into space.

My life has been enriched by having met President John F. Kennedy in Santa Monica as well as working with Sen. Robert F. Kennedy in 1968

REMEMBER CAMELOT WILL NEVER DIE.

Visiting The Robert F. Kennedy Community School

Today is September 9, 2014 and I had an opportunity to visit the RFK Community School. I was amazed at how beautiful it was. One of the faculty showed me around after I told her about working with the Kennedy campaign in 1968. I was able to vist the spot, in the library, where Bobby gave his last speech and where "The Sounds of Time" performed all night. It was a powerful experience and I promised myself not to cry as I had at the JFK library where I had gone for a special RFK memorial dialogue. It was the first time in over 45 years that I was able to stay composed. I cried in the White House, at Arlington National, and many other places. The awful impact of my 23rd birthday night has never left me.

For the first time in years Bobby and I had three straight nights of back and forth dialogue. We talked and talked as if he were there. When I woke up I felt happy. It was the kind of happiness that comes from a certain "knowing". I needed those conversations to finish my book. As soon as I made up my mind to write about my experience people came out of the woodwork to help me. You have no idea what an amazing experience this has been. Robert Kennedy was strong with those who were powerful and gentle with those who were struggling. He was gentle with those who were suffering.

THE DRAGONFLIES

After Bobby died I grabbed my guitar and caught a greyhound bus to San Francisco. Bobby Darin had been the S.F. entertainment for RFK and he tore up his hotel room when he heard the news. Darin was to northern California what we were in southern California. I wish I had met him.

One day while walking on a dusty road in Sacramento, just due south of S.F., two dragonflies flew directly in front of me at eye level and they hovered there for at least a minute. I was mesmerized. Then they did a maneuver that looked like bowing. All this time I just stood completely still in wonder.I always looked for signs and this was a big sign for my life. I felt rejuvenated and light. I have never forgotten that moment. I wondered if dragonflies could become dragons?

ONE MORE THING

Life is amazing. Just when you think you understand it – then it's time to go. Where we go depends on the actions we have taken during our brief time on this planet. Think on that.

The Kennedy brothers came into my life when I was 17 and 22 years old. I have been fortunate to meet Robert Kennedy's children and they are amazing. They love America and the world. Please say a prayer for them. Lots of prayers.

JUST THE BEGINNING

Mrs. Ethel Kennedy gave us a song to sing. "This man is your man- this man is my man - from California to the New York Islands ... and everyone loved it. Years later Paul Ziffren, of Gibson Dunn and Crutcher, became my attorney. He had helped elect President Kennedy and worked with R.F.K. He worked with me because of the work I had done on the campaign with Bobby.

Have you ever walked into a place, you have never been in, walked up to four people, who you did not know, and then introduced yourself and began to tell them their names? That is the truth and why things get amazing at times.

I was born on the day the war in Europe was declared over. What better day to be born then that. We live in a tumultuous world where there is always enough news and never enough answers. Our individual problems generally have to do with feeding and housing our families. Some countries are easier to live in then others. The middle east seems to have problems with all of the above. Imagine how great they would be if they lived in peace. I believe they would be amazing.

Bobby Kennedy loved people and wanted them to protect this earth as much as they wanted to protect their families. He loved all types of people. He connected with all of them.

That's Me. I have never stopped believing.

That picture was taken in Paris, France where I had to go to the pyranees mountains because of lung problems. Life had put me in a place.

I don't know about you but I think I looked kind of cute ☺

THE SOUNDS OF TIME, LEON-JIM-GAYLEEN- R.F.K. SINGERS

PLEASE GO TO WWW.RFK68.COM

AND LET ME KNOW THAT YOU HAVE A PHOTO OF VAIZ
MEEHR, LEON W. FAINSTADT, AND ROBERT KENNEDY.

SO MANY PEOPLE TOOK PHOTOS OF MYSELF WITH BOBBY AND WANTED
TO GIVE THEM TO ME. I DID NOT HAVE A MEANS TO PROTECT THEM.

GET IN TOUCH! I WOULD LOVE TO HAVE ONE OF THOSE PHOTOS.

I ALWAYS THOUGHT THERE WOULD BE ANOTHER DAY

ONCE AGAIN THANKS FOR GETTING THIS BOOK.

TRANSLATION: LION WOLF IN A GOOD CITY – LEON WOLF FAINSTADT

My Main Goal: World Peace

<u>Women will make it happen.</u>

<u>Women are the key to Peace</u>

PEACE: LEON W. FAINSTADT AUGUST 17, 2014

THE AMERICAN FLAG MASK WAS FIRST DESIGNED IN 1990
BY THE FREEDOM TRAIL CORP. I CREATED IT IN SUPPORT
OF AMERICAN EDUCATION. CREATED AS A LOGO WHICH
WAS EASILY IDENTIFIABLE AND USED BY "CHAMPIONS" OF
ALL CHILDREN IN AMERICA. TWO CHAMPIONS, MALE AND
FEMALE, WEAR THE MASK TO CREATE HEROIC FIGURES.

IN KEEPING WITH CREATING "RIPPLES OF HOPE" IT IS MY
BELIEF THAT ONLY THROUGH EDUCATION CAN THERE
BE A LEVEL PLAYING FIELD FOR ALL AMERICANS.

CURRENTLY THERE ARE PROBLEMS ACROSS AMERICA
IN WHICH CHILDREN AND ADULTS SUFFER. FINANCIAL
DISPARITIES. THE ENVIRONMENT SUFFERS FROM THE
INDIFFERENCE OF CAPTAINS OF INDUSTRY WHO DESTROY
MOUNTAINS AND RIVERS WITH ABANDON FOR MONEY.

FROM THAT SAD DAY IN 1968 TO THE PRESENT I HAVE
PRAYED FOR GUIDANCE ON HOW TO CREATE VALUE WITH
MY LIFE. ALL EFFORTS MOVE TOWARDS CREATING RIPPLES
OF HOPE. ROBERT F. KENNEDY IS MY CHAMPION.

SAVING OUR PLANET FROM THE HORRIBLE DESTRUCTION
OF A NUCLEAR WAR SHOULD BE THE DECISIVE FACTOR.
YOU'RE HERE BECAUSE THEY WERE HERE.

PLEASE LEARN ABOUT HAYM SALOMON

HE SAVED GEORGE WASHINGTON'S ARMY AND SUPPLIED
MONEY TO THE REVOLUTION WHENEVER IT WAS NEEDED.

HE WAS COURAGEOUS, GENEROUS, AND JEWISH.

PRESIDENT WASHINGTON NEVER FORGOT HIM.

George Washington gave a speech where he stated

The Jewish people would always be welcome in America.

I believe the generosity of Haym Salomon had a lot to do with that.

ROBERT FRANCIS KENNEDY MASS CARD

November 20, 1925 - June 6, 1968

Dear God,

Please take care of him who tried to take care of yours.

"Come, my friends,

Tis not too late to see a newer world"

- Tennyson, Ulysses

"Aeschylus wrote: 'In our sleep, pain that cannot forget falls drop by drop upon the heart and in our own despair, against our will, comes wisdom through the awful grace of God.'

"What we need in the United States ... is love and wisdom and compassion toward one another, and a feeling of justice toward those who still suffer within our own country, whether they be white or they be black.

"Let us dedicate ourselves to what the Greeks wrote so many years ago: to tame the savageness of man and make gentle the life of the world. let us dedicate ourselves to that, and say a prayer for our country and for our people."

- Robert F. Kennedy

Extemporaneous remarks on the death of Martin Luther King. Indianpolis, Indiana April 4, 1968

WHEN YOU SEE THIS SIGN YOU ARE DRIVING PAST THE
LOCATION OF THE RFK COMMUNITY SCHOOLS. THE SCHOOLS
ARE BEAUTIFUL. ONCE ON THIS SITE STOOD A MAN THAT
COULD MOVE THE WORLD AND HE AND HIS BROTHER DID JUST
THAT. RFK WAS AWESOME. AMEN.

SAY A PRAYER, CROSS YOURSELF, DRAW A STAR OF DAVID,
OR WHATEVER YOU MAY DO BUT APPRECIATE THE MAN
WHO ALLOWED YOUR FAMILIES TO BREATH FREEDOM. ONE
OF TWO AMERICANS WHO GAVE IT ALL FOR YOURSELF AND
GENERATIONS TO FOLLOW.

ONCE A WRITER FOR THE LOS ANGELES TIMES ASKED ME WHY
I LIKED ROBERT F. KENNEDY. I TOLD HIM HE REMINDED ME OF
ABRAHAM LINCOLN. HE WAS NOT SURE HOW TO RESPOND.

I TOLD JACK SMITH SEN. ROBERT KENNEDY REMINDED ME OF
LINCOLN BECAUSE HE HAD POWER BUT WAS GENTLE.

Jacqueline Olivera-Rojas, one of the principals, took me around the school to allow me to see the murals, visit the spot where our group, The Sounds of Time, performed for Bobby Kennedy.

I stood in front of a plaque that had June 5, 1968 in bronze. It spoke about the man and our time.

I found out that The Library was recently named in honor of a Paul Schrade who was instrumental in the struggle to acquire the property and to build Robert F. Kennedy Community Schools. I never had a chance to meet him but he is a very good man who supported his American Hero. He survived being shot by a bullet that awful night.

I had driven by that school often and yet this was the first time I decided to look inside. I was amazed at the beauty that I encountered.

Ms. Jacqueline Olivera-Rojas then took me to the Cocoanut Grove which was truly beautiful. I could not help thinking back to that night when THE SOUNDS OF TIME, my group performed with Andy Williams. Where I met Sen./Astronaut John Glenn on stage and listened to Robert Kennedy charm the crowd.

It was a great time and then time ran out for the man we loved.

I have two footballs that I keep in the living room of my place. One is for President Kennedy and the other for Robert F. Kennedy. Two people that will never be replaced.

It has taken me 46 years to write this book. I was hoping someone else would write this book but then the only people that really wrote anything about the Kennedy family generally wrote from the outside looking in. I pray for all the family and our country to get better.

For additional information, visit the author's website:

www.rfk68.com